*The Crisp Approach to*

# getting creative
# with newsletters in
# WORDPERFECT

by Sandy Zook

The
*Crisp
Computer*
Series

Editor: David Foster
Project Manager: David Foster
Interior Design: Kathleen Gadway
Cover Design: Kathleen Gadway

Library of Congress No 93-70805

ISBN 1-56052-219-4

WordPerfect is the registered trademark of WordPerfect Corporation.

# Crisp Computer Book Series

These books are not like other books. Inspired by the widely successful "Fifty-Minute" Crisp Books, these books provide the least you need to know in order to use today's most popular application software packages. Specifically designed for either self-study or business training, they are "the fifty-minute books that teach!"

These guides are not for technical wizards or power users. They are for the average business person who is not familiar with computers nor comfortable with a particular software package—such as WordPerfect, Lotus 1-2-3, or Excel.

In most everyday computer applications, employees, managers, and students do not need to learn every feature and capability of their software. What most business users want is simply the amount of knowledge—delivered as quickly and painlessly as possible—to perform specific duties: write the letter, report or newsletter; create the budget or sales forecast; set up a mailing list; and other important business tasks. These books use everyday business examples to guide readers step-by-step through just those commands that they will use most.

Concise and practical, the Crisp fifty-minute computer books provide quick, easy ways to learn today's most popular computer software applications.

# Other Books in the Crisp Computer Series

*Beginning DOS for Nontechnical Business Users*
Gordon Kimbell
ISBN: 1-56052-212-7

*Beginning Lotus for Nontechnical Business Users*
L.Louise Van Osdol
ISBN: 1-56052-213-5

*Beginning WordPerfect 5.1 for Nontechnical Business Users*
Mark Workman
ISBN: 1-56052-214-3

*Beginning Excel for Nontechnical Business Users*
William Amadio
ISBN: 1-56052-215-1

*DOS for WordPerfect Users*
Pamela Mills and Barbara Mathias
ISBN: 1-56052-216-X

*WordPerfect Styles Made Easy*
Geraldine Mosher
ISBN: 1-56052-217-8

*WordPerfect Sorting Made Easy*
Patricia Fordham
ISBN: 1-56052-218-6

# Contents

## Lesson 3  Welcome to Design: The Keystrokes  29

# To the Reader

*Getting Creative with Newsletters in WordPerfect* is a book of artistic and imaginative newsletters for people with little or no desktop publishing experience. Its purpose is to help you create a variety of newsletters—with all of the necessary WordPerfect keystrokes broken down into short, explicit segments, as well as explanations to help you incorporate any of the ideas into your own publications.

The examples in this book were produced in an easy, uncomplicated format. If an example seems too complicated for you at the moment, try it again later. As you learn new skills, the example that *was* too complicated will soon make sense. And, as your WordPerfect desktop publishing knowledge expands, you will generate far more sophisticated newsletters than the ones created in this book.

Your first newsletter will probably take longer to create than you plan. However, taking the time to learn a product that you will continue to use is *not* a waste of time; it is a time saver. So, allow twice as much time for learning, experimenting and setting up styles—the pressure of a deadline can take the fun away.

Express yourself: draw up a plan; find a similar example in the book; and enter the codes, keystrokes or ideas into your documents for practical, great-looking newsletters.

You do not need a laser printer to enjoy this book, although a laser printer is preferable. All of the keystrokes were created using WordPerfect and a Panasonic KX-P4430 laser printer that is compatible with the HP LaserJet III. Scalable fonts are almost imperative for creating good-looking documents. Soft fonts (printing programs that expand your selection of typefaces) range from $30 to $150 for dot-matrix and laser printers alike.

## Basic Design and Layout

This book does not teach design as a topic by itself. It does, however, incorporate fundamental design concepts into the many examples so that you can decide what works best for you.

The important point to remember is that convincing messages (newsletters, advertisements, financial reports) combine appearance and content (looks as well as words). Your newsletter should send a message in a way that makes it easy for readers to comprehend that message. The design should not be noticed. How fast and effectively you convey your information is the accomplishment of your graphic composition.

## WordPerfect's Help Phone Numbers

If you experience difficulty working with WordPerfect, you can call 1-800-321-5096 (features), 1-800-321-3383 (graphics), or 1-800-321-5170 (laser printers). If there is a bug in the program, you'll get a free update. If the problem is your fault, they will help you. Either way, you'll get something for your troubles.

I hope *Getting Creative with Newsletters in WordPerfect* will serve as both a starting point and an ongoing reference book. My goal has been to make it easy and enjoyable for you to make the most of WordPerfect's desktop publishing features.

Sandy Zook, Author

# 1

# Getting Started

Before you create your first newsletter, it is essential to set up and use a few time-saving functions. One of these functions is creating separate directories on your disk to categorize and store your keyboards, macros, graphics, and documents for easy retrieval and backup. A directory is an area on your disk to hold files.

If you do not create these new directories and change your *Setup* (**Shift-F1**), WordPerfect will automatically store your newly created macros and newsletters in the current default directory. If you then change directories, WordPerfect will not be able to find or execute your macros.

# Create DOS Directories

## Create a DOS Directory to Store Your Documents

Do this section only if your documents are not already separated.

1.  Start at the blank editing screen
2.  Press *List* (**F5**), then press **Enter** to access your current directory
3.  Keep your cursor on **. Current <dir>**
4.  Choose **O**ther Directory (7)
5.  Type a directory name and press **Enter**
    For example, **C:\WPDOC**
6.  Choose **Y**es to create a new directory
7.  Press *Exit* (**F7**) to return to the editing screen

## Create a Directory for C:\WPDOC\MACROS

Do this section only if you do not have your macros already separated.

1.  Press *List* (**F5**) and then press **Enter** to access your current directory
2.  Keep your cursor on **. Current <dir>**
3.  Choose **O**ther Directory (7)
4.  Type a directory name and press **Enter**
    For example, **C:\WPDOC\MACROS**
5.  Choose **Y**es to create a new directory
6.  Press *Exit* (**F7**) to return to the editing screen

## Create a Directory for C:\WPDOC\NEWSLETR

1. Press *List* (**F5**) and press **Enter** to access your current directory
2. Keep your cursor on **. Current <dir>**
3. Choose **O**ther Directory (7)
4. Type a directory name and press **Enter**
   For example, **C:\WPDOC\NEWSLETR**
5. Choose **Y**es to create a new directory
6. Press *Exit* (**F7**) to return to the editing screen

You want the documents you create to be in a separate directory for easy backup as well as retrieval. You do not need, however, to back up graphics because they are already on a disk. That is why Graphics is a subdirectory under C:\WP51 instead of C:\WPDOC.

## Create a Directory for C:\WP51\GRAPHICS

Do this only if you have not already separated your graphics files.

1. Press *List* (**F5**) and press **Enter** to access your current directory
2. Keep your cursor on **. Current <dir>**
3. Choose **O**ther Directory (7)
4. Type a directory name and press **Enter**
   For example, **C:\WP51\GRAPHICS**
5. Choose **Y**es to create a new directory
6. Press *Exit* (**F7**) to return to the editing screen

So far, you have only *created* the DOS directories. Now, you need to tell WordPerfect that you have these directories. (Again, only change the directory names if you have not done so previously.)

### Tell WordPerfect You Have Special MACROS, GRAPHICS, and NEWSLETR Directories

1. Press *Setup* (**Shift-F1**)

2. Choose **L**ocation of Files (6)

3. Choose **K**eyboard/Macro Files (2)

4. Type the name of your macro directory, **C:\WPDOC\MACROS**, and press **Enter**

5. Choose **G**raphic Files (6)

6. Type the name of your graphics directory, **C:\WP51\GRAPHICS**, and press **Enter**

7. Choose **D**ocument Files (7)

8. Type the name of your document directory, **C:\WPDOC\NEWSLETR**, and press **Enter**

9. Press *Exit* (**F7**) to return to the editing screen

From now on, WordPerfect will store all new document files in the new C:\WPDOC\NEWSLETR directory and new macros in the C:\WPDOC\MACROS directory. If you have another directory for documents, you will have to change directories to find your old files.

## Move the Current Files

### Move Soft Keyboards, Macros, and Graphics to Their Respective Directories

WordPerfect came with some graphics, shortcut macros, and soft keyboards. You need to move them to their new respective DOS directory. Also, if you created some macros and did not specify a directory, you will need to move them as well.

## Move WordPerfect Soft Keyboards

Do the following only if your soft keyboards are mixed in with your WordPerfect programs.

1. Press *List* (**F5**) to see **Dir C:\WPDOC\NEWSLETR\*.***
2. Change what you see to **C:\WP51\*.WPK** and press **Enter**
3. Press *Mark Text* (**Alt-F5**) to mark an * by all keyboard file names
4. Choose **M**ove/Rename (3)
5. Choose **Y**es to accept all marked files
6. At Move marked files to:, type **C:\WPDOC\MACROS** and press **Enter**
7. Press *Exit* (**F7**) to return to the editing screen

## Move WordPerfect Macros

Do the following only if your macros are mixed in with your WordPerfect programs.

1. Press *List* (**F5**) to see **Dir C:\WPDOC\NEWSLETR\*.***
2. Change what you see to **C:\WP51\*.WPM** and press **Enter**
3. Press *Mark Text* (**Alt-F5**) to mark an * by all macro file names
4. Choose **M**ove/Rename (3)
5. Choose **Y**es to move all marked files
6. At Move marked files to:, type **C:\WPDOC\MACROS** and press **Enter**
7. Press *Exit* (**F7**) to return to the editing screen

## Move WordPerfect Graphics

Do the following only if your graphic files are mixed in with your WordPerfect programs.

1. Press *List* (**F5**) to see **Dir C:\WPDOC\NEWSLETR\*.***
2. Change what you see to **C:\WP51\*.WPG** and press **Enter**
3. Press *Mark Text* (**Alt-F5**) to mark an * by all macro file names
4. Choose **M**ove/Rename (3)
5. Choose **Y**es to move all marked files
6. At Move marked files to:, type **C:\WP51\GRAPHICS** and press **Enter**
7. Press *Exit* (**F7**) to return to the editing screen

## Move Your Other Documents

Do the following only if your other documents are mixed in with your WordPerfect programs.

1. Press *List* (**F5**) to see **Dir C:\WPDOC\NEWSLETR\*.***
2. Change what you see to **C:\WP51\*.*** and press **Enter**
3. Type an * by the documents that *you* created, *not* program files

   **NOTE:** If you typed an * by the name of a file you do not want to move, type an * by the filename again to remove it.

4. Choose **M**ove/Rename (3)
5. Choose **Y**es to move all marked files
6. At Move marked files to:, type **C:\WPDOC** and press **Enter**
7. Press *Exit* (**F7**) to return to the editing screen

# Notes

# Notes

_____

_____

_____

_____

_____

_____

_____

_____

_____

_____

_____

_____

_____

_____

_____

_____

_____

_____

_____

_____

_____

_____

# 2

# Creating and Using Keyboards

"Soft" keyboards are another timesaving WordPerfect feature. A soft keyboard is a file that stores shortcut keys. Some of the shortcuts have been created by WordPerfect; you will create others as you need them.

WordPerfect comes with six soft keyboards. In this section you will take the best parts of each keyboard that came with WordPerfect and create your own personalized soft keyboard. WordPerfect allows you to program your keyboard using different soft keyboards for different occasions. You can have a soft keyboard for daily routines, another for corporate reports, and yet another for newsletters.

Keyboard macros are faster than macro files because the keyboard macros have already been loaded into memory.

You can create macros to switch between keyboards and assign the macros to the same keys on all your keyboards. For example, **Ctrl-N** might be your newsletter keyboard, and **Ctrl-C** might be your corporate report keyboard.

## WordPerfect's Ready-Made Soft Keyboards

ALTRNAT.WPK
EQUATION.WPK
MACROS.WPK
SHORTCUT.WPK
FASTKEYS.WPK
ENHANCED.WPK

# General Keyboard Information

## Copy One Keyboard to Another Keyboard

This should be done before editing in case you ever want the use
the original again.

1. Press *Setup* (**Shift-F1**)

2. Choose **K**eyboard Layout (5)

3. Move your cursor to the keyboard you want to copy
   In this case, move your cursor to SHORTCUT

4. Look at the bottom of the screen

5. Choose Cop**y** (5)

6. Type the new keyboard name and press **Enter**
   For example, type **SANDY**

   **NOTE:** The keyboards are in alphabetical order.

7. Press *Exit* (**F7**) to return to the editing screen

## Rename a Keyboard

1. Press *Setup* (**Shift-F1**)

2. Choose **K**eyboard Layout (5)

3. Move your cursor to the keyboard you want to rename
   For example, move to SANDY

4. Choose **R**ename (3)

5. Type the new keyboard name and press **Enter**
   For example, type **YOURNAME**

## Delete a Keyboard

While still in the Setup:Keyboard Layout menu,

1. Move your cursor to the keyboard you want to delete
   In this case, move to YOURNAME

2. Choose **D**elete (2)

3. Choose **Y**es to confirm deletion

## Look at the Key Assignments of an Existing Keyboard

While still in the Setup:Keyboard Layout menu,

1. Move your cursor to the keyboard you want to look at
   For example, move to MACROS

2. Choose **E**dit (7)

3. Use your **Up Arrow** (↑) or **Down Arrow** (↓) to see the key assignments

4. Press *Cancel* (**F1**), **Y**es to cancel and *not* save any changes, and return to the keyboard layout screen

## Look at the Map of an Existing Keyboard

While still in the Setup:Keyboard Layout menu,

1. Move your cursor to the keyboard you want to map
   For example, SHORTCUT

2. Choose **M**ap (8)

3. Use the **Left Arrow** (←), **Right Arrow** (→), **Up Arrow** (↑), or **Down Arrow** (↓) to see the key assignments

   Notice the Key, Action, and Description fields at the bottom of the screen as you move your cursor, especially when your cursor is on the **Alt** or **Ctrl** key action area.

## Go to a Specific Key on the Keyboard Map

While still in the Keyboard:Map screen:

1. Press **N** for Name Search, then type what you want to see
   For example, press **Ctrl-C** to move your cursor to that key

2. Press **N** for Name Search
   For example, press **Alt-L** to move your cursor to that key

3. Press *Cancel* (**F1**), **Y**es to cancel and *not* save any changes, and return to the keyboard layout screen

4. Press *Exit* (**F7**) to return to the editing screen

## Select a Previously Created Keyboard Layout

The macros already created in this keyboard will take precedence over your macros, meaning that you will eventually want to change some of the programmed keys to make use of WordPerfect macros.

1. Press *Setup* (**Shift-F1**)

2. Choose **K**eyboard Layout (5)

3. Move your cursor to the keyboard you want to use
      In this case, move to FASTKEYS

4. Choose **S**elect (1)

   Notice the keyboard name next to Keyboard Layout.

5. Press *Exit* (**F7**) to return to the editing screen

## Exercise

1. Press **Ctrl-D** for date text

2. Press **Ctrl-K** for copy and follow the instructions on the screen

3. Press **Ctrl-P** for print preview

4. Press *Exit* (**F7**) to return to the editing screen when finished

## Return to the Original WordPerfect Keyboard

There are two ways to select the original keyboard:

1. Press **Ctrl-6** (not **F6**) or

Use the menu to return to the original WordPerfect keyboard:

1. Press *Setup* (**Shift-F1**)

2. Choose **K**eyboard Layout (5)

3. Choose **O**riginal (6)

   Notice that there is no keyboard name.

4. Press *Exit* (**F7**)to return to the editing screen

You can press **Ctrl-6** to toggle between the original WordPerfect keyboard and the last keyboard selected. However, sometimes the toggle feature doesn't work.

## Create a New Keyboard Layout from Scratch

1. Press *Setup* (**Shift-F1**)

2. Choose **K**eyboard Layout (5)

3. Choose **C**reate (4)

4. Type the name of your new keyboard (up to 8 characters) and press **Enter**

    For example, type **WHATEVER**

5. Choose **E**dit (7)

    At this point, this soft keyboard has no special keys. You could add the keys one by one, but it would be faster to start with some keys that have already been programmed, and then delete or rename the keys you don't want.

6. Press *Exit* (**F7**) to exit the Keyboard:Edit screen

7. Press *Exit* (**F7**) to exit the Setup:Keyboard Layout menu and return to the editing screen

# Create Your NEWSLETR Soft Keyboard

Create a soft keyboard using the following keys. Some of the keys contain symbols, others are ready-made macros (actions) from other soft keyboards that came with WordPerfect. The **Alt**-character keys are left blank so that you can use them for your favorite macros.

Do not type this list now. It lists the keys that you will program later in this lesson.

| | |
|---|---|
| **Ctrl-A** | Format:Other:Advance |
| **Ctrl-B** | Reserved for Page # |
| **Ctrl-C** | © (Copyright) symbol |
| **Ctrl-D** | Current Date Text |
| **Ctrl-E** | Edit a Code |
| **Ctrl-F** | Font:Base Font |
| **Ctrl-G** | Graphics:Figure:Create |
| **Ctrl-H** | ½ (One-Half) symbol |
| **Ctrl-I** | Italics |
| **Ctrl-J** | Format:Line:Justification |
| **Ctrl-K** | Superscript |
| **Ctrl-L** | ☜ (Left-Pointing Finger) symbol |
| **Ctrl-M** | ™ (Trade Mark) symbol |
| **Ctrl-N** | ® (Registered Trademark) symbol |
| **Ctrl-O** | □ (Empty Box) symbol |
| **Ctrl-P** | Print:View |
| **Ctrl-Q** | ¼ (One-Quarter) symbol |
| **Ctrl-R** | ☞ (Right-Pointing Finger) symbol |
| **Ctrl-S** | Small text |
| **Ctrl-T** | ☎ (Telephone) symbol |
| **Ctrl-U** | ★ (Star) symbol |
| **Ctrl-V** | Reserved for Compose key |
| **Ctrl-W** | ✓ (Check Mark) symbol |
| **Ctrl-X** | Extra Large |
| **Ctrl-Y** | Very Large |
| **Ctrl-Z** | Large |
| ' | " (Opening, or Left Quote) symbol |
| ~ | " (Closing, or Right Quote) symbol |

## Copy the SHORTCUT Keyboard to a Keyboard Called NEWSLETR

This keeps the original intact so that it will still be there if you want to start over, or if you want to create another keyboard based on the original SHORTCUT keyboard.

1. Press *Setup* (**Shift-F1**)
2. Choose **K**eyboard Layout (5)
3. Move your cursor to the keyboard you want to copy
    In this case, move the cursor to SHORTCUT
4. Choose Cop**y** (5)
5. Type the new keyboard name, **NEWSLETR**, and press **Enter**

## Edit the Keyboard

1. Move your cursor to the keyboard you want to work with
    In this case, NEWSLETR
2. Choose **E**dit (7)

## Delete a Macro Definition from a Key (change back to original definition)

1. Use your arrow keys to move the cursor to **Alt-R** (the key you want to delete)
2. Choose **O**riginal (3)
3. Press **Y**es to verify

Now we'll repeat those steps to delete a second macro definition.

1. Use your arrow keys to move your cursor to **Alt-A** (the key you want to delete)
2. Choose **O**riginal (3)
3. Press **Y**es to verify

## Exercise

Continue to delete the following key definitions. Some of the keys you are deleting will be useful on another soft keyboard but not on the one you are creating now. You will need some of the keys left blank by these deletions for other functions.

| | |
|---|---|
| Alt-W | Ctrl-T |
| Alt-B | Ctrl-H |
| Alt-F | Ctrl-I |
| Alt-G | Ctrl-J |
| Alt-O | Ctrl-L |
| Alt-T | Ctrl-M |
| Ctrl-C | Ctrl-O |
| Ctrl-D | Ctrl-P |
| Ctrl-E | Ctrl-Q |
| Ctrl-F | Ctrl-S |

Press **Home, Home, Up Arrow** (↑) to see a full listing of the keys that remain. They are listed below.

| | |
|---|---|
| Alt-E | Alt-I |
| Alt-P | Alt-S |
| Alt-D | Alt-L |
| Alt-X | Alt-V |
| Ctrl-B | Ctrl-G |

## Accident—Deleted Wrong Key?

You can either:

- Cancel the whole process and start again by pressing *Cancel* (**F1**), then **Y**es or
- Copy the key again from the SHORTCUT keyboard

To copy a key from the SHORTCUT keyboard to the NEWSLETR keyboard

- Press *Exit* (**F7**) to exit the Keyboard:Edit screen

# Copy a Key Definition to Another Keyboard

## General Ideas

In the **source** keyboard (the keyboard that has the key you want),

- Save the key definition to a macro (.WPM) file, then
- Edit the **destination** keyboard (the keyboard where you want to send the key) and assign the newly created macro (.WPM) file to a key definition.

## Specific Keystrokes

**The source keyboard:** How to save the key definition to a macro. (Have your cursor at the Setup:Keyboard Layout menu.)

1. Move your cursor to the keyboard that has the key you want
   For example, SHORTCUT

2. Press <u>E</u>dit (7)

3. Move your cursor to the key you want to send
   For example, **Ctrl-J**

4. Choose <u>S</u>ave (6)

5. At Define macro:, type **TEMP** and press **Enter**

   You can enter a macro name that is up to 8 characters long, or press **Alt+character**. WordPerfect will add the **.WPM** extension and put the macro in the macro directory. If the macro already exists, WordPerfect will alert you.

6. Press *Exit* (**F7**) to exit the Keyboard:Edit screen

**The destination keyboard:** Assign a macro to a key definition.

1. Move your cursor to the keyboard you want to send a macro to

   For example, NEWSLETR

2. Choose **E**dit (7)

3. Press **R**etrieve (7)

4. At Key:, press **Ctrl-J**

   Use the key combination **Alt**+character or **Ctrl**+character for the new key assignment.

5. At Macro:, type **TEMP** and press **Enter**

   Type the macro name you want in your keyboard.

## Rename a Key

Rename all of the **Alt-**character keys because you will need them to create regular macros. Also, you might have previously created macros; the programmed **Alt-**character keys in the soft keyboard you see now take precedence over regular macros, thus making your earlier macros inaccessible.

1. Use your arrow keys to move the cursor to **Alt-D**, the key you want to rename

2. Choose **M**ove (5)

3. At Key:, press **Ctrl-D** for the new name

   If the key combination has *not* been used, then the old key actions will have a new name. If the key combination *has* been used, WordPerfect asks if you want to delete the old one so you can use its name. Press **Y**es to verify.

## Exercise

Do *not* use **Ctrl-V**; **Ctrl-V** is reserved for the Compose key. Also, do *not* use **Ctrl-B**; **Ctrl-B** is reserved for page numbers.

Press **Home**, **Home**, then **Up Arrow** (↑) to go to the top of the list and rename:

| | | |
|---|---|---|
| Move cursor to **Alt-P** | Choose <u>M</u>ove (**5**) | Press **Ctrl-K** (not P) |
| Move cursor to **Alt-E** | Choose <u>M</u>ove (**5**) | Press **Ctrl-E** |
| Move cursor to **Alt-I** | Choose <u>M</u>ove (**5**) | Press **Ctrl-I** |
| Move cursor to **Alt-S** | Choose <u>M</u>ove (**5**) | Press **Ctrl-S** |
| Move cursor to **Alt-L** | Choose <u>M</u>ove (**5**) | Press **Ctrl-Z** (not L) |
| Move cursor to **Alt-X** | Choose <u>M</u>ove (**5**) | Press **Ctrl-X** |
| Move cursor to **Alt-V** | Choose <u>M</u>ove (**5**) | Press **Ctrl-Y** (not V) |
| Move cursor to **Ctrl-B** | Choose <u>M</u>ove (**5**) | Press **Ctrl-F** (not B) |

---

**Keyboard:Edit**
Name: **NEWSLETR**

| Key | Action | Description |
|---|---|---|
| Ctrl-E | {KEY MACRO 15} | Edit a Code |
| Ctrl-F | {KEY MACRO 23} | Base Font |
| Ctrl-G | {KEY MACRO 17} | Graphic -create a graphic figure |
| Ctrl-I | {KEY MACRO 1} | Italics |
| Ctrl-J | {KEY MACRO 7} | Justification |
| Ctrl-K | {KEY MACRO 21} | Superscript |
| Ctrl-S | {KEY MACRO 6} | Small |
| Ctrl-X | {KEY MACRO 3} | Extra Large |
| Ctrl-Y | {KEY MACRO 4} | Very Large |
| Ctrl-Z | {KEY MACRO 5} | Large |

1 <u>A</u>ction; 2 <u>D</u>scrptn; 3 <u>O</u>riginal; 4 <u>C</u>reate; 5 <u>M</u>ove; **Macro**: 6 <u>S</u>ave; 7 <u>R</u>etrieve: 1

---

Press *Exit* (**F7**) to exit the Keyboard:Edit screen

## Add an Action to a Keyboard Key

With your cursor on the NEWSLETR keyboard,

1. Choose **E**dit (7)

2. Choose **C**reate (4)

   WordPerfect asks for the assignment key.

3. At Key:, type **Shift-~** (the tilde or diacritical mark)

4. At Description:, type **Closing (right) quote marks** and press **Enter**

   You are now at the Key:Action screen.

5. Enter the actions and type the characters you want this key to do in the Action box

   Press the **Delete** key to delete the original meaning

   Press **Ctrl-2** (not **Ctrl-V** or **Ctrl-F2**) for Compose

   Nothing appears on the screen, not even the number you just typed. As you type the following numbers, those numbers will not show on the screen either. Only after you press **Enter** will the result appear.

   Type **4,31** and press **Enter**

   A little square box appears. You can see the actual character in the *Print:View* screen.

   **NOTE:** The Action box works the same way the Macro Editor works. **Ctrl-V** allows you to add one action keystroke, **Ctrl-F10** allows you to add multiple action keystrokes, and **Ctrl-PgUp** lets you see a menu of actions and commands.

6. Press *Exit* (**F7**) to exit the Action box

## Add Another Key

1. Choose **C**reate (4)

   WordPerfect asks for the assignment key

2. At Key:, type ' (the apostrophe; not the single quote)

3. At Description:, type **Opening (left) quote marks**
   and press **Enter**

4. In the Action box, press the **Delete** key to delete the original
   meaning

5. Press **Ctrl-2** (not **Ctrl-V** or **Ctrl-F2**) for Compose

   Remember, it will look like nothing has happened.

6. Type **4,32** and press **Enter**

   As we expected, the numbers did not show as you typed.
   However, after you pressed **Enter** a little square box
   appeared.

7. Press *Exit* (**F7**) to exit the Action box

8. Press *Exit* (**F7**) again to exit the Keyboard:Edit screen

9. Choose **S**elect (1) to select the NEWSLETR keyboard

7. Press *Exit* (**F7**) and return to the editing screen

## Test Your New Key

1. Press ' for left quote

2. Type your message, **HI**

3. Press ~ for right quote

## Print View

1. Press *Print* (**Shift-F7**)

2. Choose **V**iew Document (6)

3. Choose **2**00% (2)

4. Press *Exit* (**F7**) to return to the editing screen

## Use the Map Function to Add Special Characters

WordPerfect has numerous special characters. To see a list of them, retrieve the file CHARACTR.DOC that is probably located in your C:\WP51 directory, then press *Print:View*. Some of the characters will show up as little squares on the editing screen but will print when sent to the printer. The document CHARACTR.DOC is approximately 43 pages. Another document, CHARMAP.TST, has the same characters in a grid format instead of one character per line. CHARMAP.TST has four pages.

1. Press *Setup* (**Shift-F1**)
2. Choose **K**eyboard Layout (5)
3. Move your cursor to the keyboard you want to map
   For example, NEWSLETR
4. Choose **M**ap (8)

## Change **Ctrl-Q** to become the ¼ (One-Quarter) Symbol

1. Move your cursor to the key you want to change
   Press **N** for Name search
   Press **Ctrl-Q** to move to that key
2. Choose **C**ompose (5)
3. At Key:, type **4,18** and press **Enter**
4. Choose **D**escription (3)
5. Type **One-Quarter** and press **Enter**

## Change **Ctrl-H** to Become the ½ (One-Half) Symbol

1. Move your cursor to the key you want to change
   Press **N** for Name search
   Press **Ctrl-H** to move to that key
2. Choose **C**ompose (5)

3. At Key:, type **4,17** and press **Enter**

4. Choose **D**escription (3)

5. Type **One-Half** and press **Enter**

## Change **Ctrl-C** to Become the Copyright Symbol

1. Move your cursor to the key you want to change

   Press **N** for Name search

   Press **Ctrl-C** to move to that key

2. Choose **C**ompose (5)

3. At Key:, type **4,23** and press **Enter**

4. Choose **D**escription (3)

5. Type **Copyright** and press **Enter**

## Exercise

Add the following symbol keys to the NEWSLETR keyboard. Use the same keystrokes as in the above example for the copyright, one-quarter and one-half symbols.

| Edit this key | To become this key | | |
| --- | --- | --- | --- |
| Press **N**, then | Choose **C**ompose (5), then type | | Choose **D**escription (3), then type |
| **Ctrl-L** | ☜ | 5,22 | Left pointing finger |
| **Ctrl-M** | ™ | 4,41 | Trademark |
| **Ctrl-N** | ® | 4,22 | Registered trademark |
| **Ctrl-O** | □ | 5,24 | Empty box |
| **Ctrl-R** | ☞ | 5,21 | Right pointing finger |
| **Ctrl-T** | ☎ | 5,30 | Telephone |
| **Ctrl-U** | ★ | 6,184 | Star |
| **Ctrl-W** | ✓ | 5,23 | Check mark |

## Send a Key Definition back to WordPerfect's Original Definition

1. Move your cursor to the key you want to change
2. Choose **O**riginal (4)
3. Press **Y**es to verify

## Return to the Edit Screen

1. Press *Exit* (**F7**) to exit the Keyboard Map screen
2. Choose **S**elect (1) to select the NEWSLETR keyboard
3. Press *Exit* (**F7**) to return to the editing screen

## Test Your Keyboard

1. Press all the keys that you just programmed—**Ctrl-L** through **Ctrl-W**

## Print View

1. Press *Print* (**Shift-F7**)
2. Choose **V**iew Document (6)
3. Choose **2**00% (2)
4. Press *Exit* (**F7**) to return to the editing screen

# Menu Action Keys

## Create a "Print View" Key

1. Press *Setup* (**Shift-F1**)
2. Choose **K**eyboard Layout (5)
3. Move your cursor to the keyboard you want to edit
4. Press **E**dit (7)

   It will look like **{Print}v** when you are finished.

5. Choose <u>C</u>reate (4)

6. At Key:, press **Ctrl-P**

7. At Description:, type **Print:View** and press **Enter**

8. In the Action box, press **Delete** to delete the current character

9. Press *Print* (**Shift-F7**) to show the print code {Print}

10. Type **V** for View

11. Press *Exit* (**F7**) to exit the Action box

## Create an "Advance Text" Key

WordPerfect has a function that will allow you to place text or graphics at specific locations on your paper. The Advance Text key automates that feature, which will look like **{Format}oa** when you are finished. This feature will be covered more thoroughly later.

While still in the Keyboard:Edit screen,

1. Choose <u>C</u>reate (4)

2. At Key:, press **Ctrl-A**

3. At Description:, type **Format:Other:Advance** and press **Enter**

4. In the Action box, press **Delete** to delete the current character

5. Press *Format* (**Shift-F8**) for Format code {Format}

6. Type **O** for Other

7. Type **A** for Advance

8. Press *Exit* (**F7**) to exit the Action box

## Create a "Date" Key

WordPerfect has a function that enters the current system date into your document. Creating a Date key automates that feature, which will look like **{Date/Outline}t** when you are finished.

While still in the Keyboard:Edit screen,

1. Choose **C**reate (4)
2. At Key:, press **Ctrl-D**
3. At Description:, type **Date:Text** and press **Enter**
4. In the Action box, press **Delete** to delete the current character
5. Press *Date/Outline* (**Shift-F5**) for {Date/Outline}
6. Type **T** for Text
7. Press *Exit* (**F7**) to exit the Action box
8. Press *Exit* (**F7**) to exit the Keyboard:Edit screen
9. Press *Exit* (**F7**) to exit the Setup:Keyboard:Layout screen

## Print a Listing of Keys Assigned to a Keyboard

1. Press *Setup* (**Shift-F1**)
2. Choose **K**eyboard Layout (5)
3. Move your cursor to the keyboard you want to print
4. Press **E**dit (7)
5. Press the **PrtScr** key

   You might have to press **PgDn** and **PrtScr** several times.
6. Press *Exit* (**F7**) twice to return to the editing screen

# Notes

# Desktop Publishing
# News Review

Sandy Zook, Editor
(808) 734-0808
©Computer Business
All rights reserved.

January 1, 1993      Volume 1, Number 1

# Welcome to Design

## Clarity!

**C**reate your publication for clarity and communication. Easy for me to say! There really are no rules to follow; however, there are general guidelines. The design you use to express your ideas clearly and with impact is called style. Your style should be appropriate. A child's scout bulletin might have a different look than a legal review.

Consistency both within the page and the document is needed. Identical margins, fonts and headline attributes keep the publication from being confusing and hold the reader's attention on the content instead of the design. The design really should not even be noticed by the reader.

## Consistency!

Being consistent does not mean everything is symmetrical and boring. Visual unbalance adds originality to a page and keeps the reader's attention. Each page should have a focal point that tells the readers look here first. Then balance the rest of the information and graphical elements around it. With one main point, the reader can skim, or stop and read more if the main idea is of interest. If there are too many "main" ideas then the readers tend to move on because not **one** item grabbed their attention. A headline, graphic or a large block of text can be used as a focal point.

### Balance

Depending on the emphasis, each graphic element you place in your publication should be in balance with the size of your page and other graphic elements. These graphic elements include pictures, sidebars, text boxes and even your masthead. If all of the graphic elements were of the same size, the reader wouldn't know which one is the most important or which one to look at first.

## Experiment!

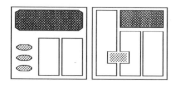

These are thumbnail sketches with facing pages (Spread).

Experiment, Experiment. Outstanding design is usually the result of trial and error. Eventually the trial and error does become less as you master your own style. Try sketching the layout on paper first. This is called a thumbnail sketch. Then do a few rough drafts on the computer. Save each try in a separate file, in case the next layout is not as good as the previous layout.

# 3

# Welcome to Design:
# The Keystrokes

## Getting Started

For your newsletter, you will use styles, soft keyboards, advance codes, shaded text boxes, graphic boxes that have text superimposed on them, and—of course—fonts. All the keystrokes and reasons for using the various ones are included, as well as the pitfalls of those that seem logical, but don't quite work.

A newsletter is divided into sections. The masthead is the title of the newsletter and is placed most often at the top or the side of the first page. The masthead is not to be confused with the headline, which is the primary title of the articles. The dateline is where the date, volume, and number of the issue are located.

## Removing a Default Library

WordPerfect comes with a style library that is sometimes set as a default. You will create your own style library.

1. Press *Setup* (**Shift-F1**)

2. Choose **L**ocation of Files (6)

3. Choose **St**yle Files (5)

4. Press **Enter** on the style directory

5. Delete any style name that appears on the second line

6. Press **Enter**

7. At Selection: **0**, press *Exit* (**F7**) to return to your document

## Clear the Current Style Library of All Old Styles

1. Press *Style* (**Alt-F8**)

   If there are no styles, press *Exit* (**F7**) and move to **Use Your NEWSLETR Keyboard...**

2. Position the cursor on the style to be deleted

3. Choose **D**elete (5)

4. Choose **D**efinition Only (3)

5. Continue to delete all style names you do not want, then

6. Press *Exit* (**F7**) when you are finished

## Use Your NEWSLETR Keyboard Created in Lesson 2

If you did not create the soft keyboard called NEWSLETR, then either return to Lesson 2 and create it or select the SHORTCUT keyboard that came with WordPerfect.

### Select a Soft Keyboard

1. Press *Setup* (**Shift-F1**)

2. Choose **K**eyboard (5)

3. Move your cursor to NEWSLETR (preferably) or SHORTCUT

4. Choose **S**elect (1)

5. Press *Exit* (**F7**)

# Create a Style for the Masthead

Selecting an open style for the masthead means that any formatting code you enter will be in effect as if you had placed it in the document directly. In a paired style code, the codes that surround the blocked text, if turned off, have no effect on any text after the [Style Off] code. An example of a paired code is the [BOLD] [bold] code. An example of an open code is the *Format:Margin* code.

## Create an Open Style

1. Press *Style* (**Alt-F8**)

2. Choose **C**reate (3)

3. Choose **N**ame (1)

4. Type **Masthead** and press **Enter**

5. Choose **T**ype (2)

6. Choose **O**pen (2)

7. Choose **D**escription (3)

    This option lets you enter a reminder of what the style does, and can be up to 54 characters long.

8. Type **Graphic w/Overlaid text, Text box w/Company data** and press **Enter**

9. Choose **C**odes (4) to format the masthead

## Store Keystrokes for Masthead into the Style

You should be in the Style (codes) screen.

## Set the Margins ½" All Around

1. Press *Format* (**Shift-F8**)

2. Choose **P**age (2)

   You should be at the Format:Page menu.

3. Choose **M**argins (5)

4. Type **.5** and press **Enter**

5. Type **1/2** and press **Enter**

   **NOTE:** You can use either decimals or fractions when you enter a unit of measure.

6. At Selection: <u>0</u>, press **Enter** to exit the Format:Page screen and return to the Format screen

   **NOTE:** If you press *Exit* (**F7**), you will return to your document. By pressing **Enter**, you go only one menu level backward. If you pressed *Exit* (**F7**) by mistake and are now in the editing screen, press *Format* (**Shift-F8**) to get back on track.

7. Choose **L**ine (1)

   You should be at the Format:Line menu.

8. Choose **M**argins (7)

9. Type **1/2** and press **Enter**

10. Type **.5** and press **Enter**

11. Choose **J**ustification (3)

12. Choose **F**ull (3)

13. Press *Exit* (**F7**) to exit the Format menu and return to the Style: (codes) screens

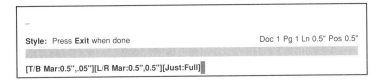

## Set the Options for the Graphic Border

1.  Press *Graphics* (**Alt-F9**)

2.  Choose **F**igure (1)

3.  Choose **O**ptions (4)

4.  Choose **B**order Style (1)

    Type **N** for none four times

5.  Choose **O**utside Border Space (2)

    Type **0** (zero) and press **Enter** (repeat four times)

6.  Choose **I**nside Border Space (3)

    Type **0** (zero) and press **Enter** (repeat four times)

    Your cursor should now be at Selection: 0

7.  Press *Exit* (**F7**) to exit the Options:Figure menu

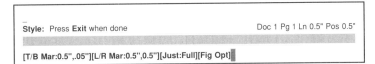

## Add the Graphic

Make sure your cursor is beyond the [Fig Opt] code. The options must be entered first or the graphic will not know about them.

1.  Press **Ctrl-G** from either soft keyboard

    **NOTE:** This the same as pressing *Graphics* (**Alt-F9**), then choosing **F**igure (1), **C**reate (1).

    You should be at the Definition:Figure menu.

2.  Choose **C**ontents (2)

3.  Choose Graphic on **D**isk (2)

    There are two ways to insert graphics into a document. One way is to retrieve a graphic and have it become a part of your

33

document. The other way is to tell WordPerfect where the graphic is so that, when it comes time to print, WordPerfect will print the graphic from the disk. With this style of inserting graphics, your document takes less disk space; but you must not remove your graphic or move it to another location or WordPerfect will be unable to print it.

 **NOTE:** This graphic must remain on the disk because style sheets cannot hold graphics. You must tell WordPerfect that the graphic will remain on the disk before you acknowledge what graphic you want.

4.  Choose **F**ilename (1)

5.  Choose *List* (**F5**) and press **Enter**

6.  Highlight the picture you want
    For example, BORD-SMR.WPG, a graphic that came with the WordPerfect's Holiday/Leisure Clip Art pack.

7.  Choose **R**etrieve (1)

    You should be at the Definition:Figure menu.

## Adjust Position and Size of the Graphics Image

1.  Choose **H**orizontal Position (6)

    Choose **L**eft (1)

2.  Choose **S**ize (7)

    Choose Set **B**oth (3)

    Type **6** for the width and press **Enter**

    Type **2** for the height and press **Enter**

3.  Choose **W**rap Text Around Box (8), and select **N**o

 **NOTE:** This is because you want to superimpose words on the graphic.

## Scale the Graphics Image

The figure is smaller than the space allowed. Scale and distort the size of your graphic until it fits the needed space. Continue to change the scale until your figure fits.

You are still in the Figure:Definition menu, but you are going to the Graphics edit screen.

1. Choose Edit (9)

2. Choose Scale (2)

3. Type **241** and press **Enter** for Scale X (width)

   The number 241 made my picture fit nicely; however your number may be different.

4. Type **106** and press **Enter** for Scale Y (height)

   Your height number may be different. Continue to adjust the scale until you find a good fit.

5. Press *Exit* (**F7**) to exit the Graphics edit screen

6. At Selection: 0, press *Exit* (**F7**) to exit the Definition:Figure menu and return to the Style (codes) screen

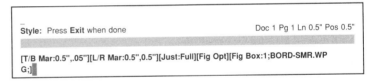

```
Style:  Press Exit when done                          Doc 1 Pg 1 Ln 0.5" Pos 0.5"

[T/B Mar:0.5",.05"][L/R Mar:0.5",0.5"][Just:Full][Fig Opt][Fig Box:1;BORD-SMR.WP
G;]
```

## Create a Box Without a Border for Company Data

1. Press **Ctrl-G** for Graphics from either soft keyboard

   **NOTE:** This the same as pressing *Graphics* (**Alt-F9**), then choosing Figure (1), Create (1).

   You are now at the Definition:Figure menu.

2. Choose Horizontal Position (6)

   Choose Right (2) (default)

3. Choose **S**ize (7), then

Choose Set **B**oth (3)

Type **1.5** for Width and press **Enter**

Type **2** for Height and press **Enter**

 **NOTE:** The size of the text box depends on the size of your paper, minus your margins, minus the width of your graphic (8.5" paper - 1" margins - 6" graphic = 1.5").

4. Choose **W**rap Text Around Box (8) and select **Y**es (default)

The Company data was placed in a graphics box with no borders. You do want all *other* text to wrap around this borderless box.

## Enter the Text for the Company Data Box

1. Choose **E**dit (9)

2. Press **Enter** three times to force the lines of text down

## Select Font for the Company Data Text

1. If you have the NEWSLETR keyboard, press **Ctrl-F**; otherwise press *Font* (**Ctrl-F8**) and choose **F**ont (4)

2. Move your cursor to CG Times (Scalable)

3. Choose **S**elect (1)

4. At Point Size:, type **9** and press **Enter**

5. Press *Flush Right* (**Alt-F6**)

6. Type your name, then **Editor**, and press **Enter**

7. Press *Flush Right* (**Alt-F6**)

8. Type your phone number and press **Enter**

9. Press *Flush Right* (**Alt-F6**)

10. Add the copyright symbol (©)

If you have the NEWSLETR keyboard, press **Ctrl-C**; otherwise press **Ctrl-V**, then at Key:, type **4,23** and press **Enter**.

 **NOTE:** The symbol will look like a box on the edit screen, but it will be visible in *Print:View* mode.

11. Type in your company name and press **Enter**

   **NOTE:** A long name might wordwrap. If it does, adjust accordingly; you have plenty of height, but not much width.

12. Press *Flush Right* (**Alt-F6**)

13. Type **All rights reserved**

14. Press *Exit* (**F7**) to exit the Graphics box edit screen and return to the Definition:Figure menu

15. Press *Exit* (**F7**) to exit the Definition:Figure menu and return to the Style (codes) screen

16. Press **Enter** so the text and graphic are not on the same line

   You will now see a partial box labelled "Fig. 2." To keep the computer's response time as fast as possible, WordPerfect does not draw the image. You can see it, however, in *Print:View* mode.

   WordPerfect will not show the text on the *Print:View* screen if you used an [Adv] code on the same line as the graphic. It will print correctly; it just won't show in *Print:View*. Since you will be using the [Adv] feature, adding the [HRt] will give you the advantage of being able to view the text without effecting its placement.

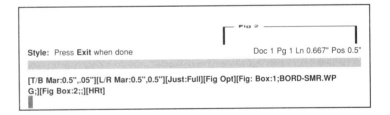

## Check Your Work

You can exit the Masthead style at any time, look at the results in *Print:View*, then return to where you left off. The following instructions describe how to do this.

## Exit Styles

1. Press *Exit* (**F7**) twice (once to exit the Styles (codes) screen and once to exit the Styles:Edit menu)

2. Choose **O**n (1) to place the masthead on your paper

   Choose **O**n just once, no matter how many times you go in and out of your style to edit it. If you press **O**n more than once, you will have the masthead in your document more than once. If that happens, delete the second style code from your editing screen.

   You are now at the editing screen. If you do not see the codes, press *Reveal Codes* (**F11** or **Alt-F3**).

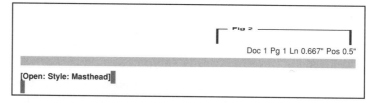

## Print View

1. Press *Print* (**Shift-F7**)

2. Choose **V**iew (6)

3. Choose 200% (2)

4. Press **Ctrl-Home, Right Arrow** (→) to see the right edge of the document and the copyright symbol

5. Choose 100% (1) to see the top half of the page

6. Press *Exit* (**F7**) to return to the editing screen

   Use the **Right Arrow** (→) to move the cursor beyond your code. You will see [Open style:Masthead]. If you place the cursor on the [Open style:Masthead] code, it will expand so you can see what is inside the code. At this point, the placement of your cursor doesn't matter.

## Edit and Add Codes to Masthead Style

1. Press *Style* (**Alt-F8**)

2. Highlight the Masthead style

3. Choose **E**dit (4)

4. Choose **C**odes (4)

5. Press **Home**, **Home**, **Down Arrow** (↓) to position your cursor beyond all the codes

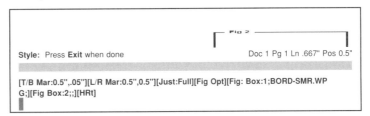

**Style:** Press **Exit** when done          Doc 1 Pg 1 Ln .667" Pos 0.5"

[T/B Mar:0.5",.05"][L/R Mar:0.5",0.5"][Just:Full][Fig Opt][Fig: Box:1;BORD-SMR.WP G;][Fig Box:2;;][HRt]

# Continue with the Masthead Style

## Add the Font for the Shadow Text

1. If you have the NEWSLETR keyboard, press **Ctrl-F**; otherwise press *Font* (**Ctrl-F8**) and choose **F**ont (4)

2. Move the cursor to Univers Bold Italic (Scalable)

3. Choose **S**elect (1)

4. At Point size:, type **20** and press **Enter**

## Color Printing

The shadow effect you see for the text "Desktop Publishing" will only work with a printer that has PCL-5 language--the HP LaserJet III, IV, or compatibles. You can also use a soft font program that is compatible with the PCL-5 printer language. If you choose a color other than black, each color will print in a different shade of gray. What you see in the example is green text (gray) with the same text printed in black slightly lower and to the left.

Red     Green    **Blue**    Yellow
Magenta    Cyan Orange    Gray
Brown    other 10 10 0

1. Press *Font* (**Ctrl-F8**)

2. Choose Print **C**olor (5)

   Notice the 0 (zero) percentages for black at the current color line.

3. Choose **G**reen (4)

   It looks like nothing has happened, but notice the percentages at the color line; green changed to 67%.

4. Press *Exit* (**F7**) to exit the Print Color menu

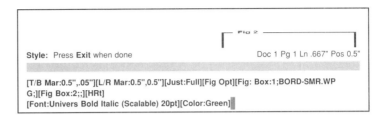

## Position the Words "Desktop Publishing" in a Specific Location

WordPerfect has a feature called *Advance* that allows you to place text anywhere on your paper regardless of where your cursor is currently located. (You might want to use your ruler for your measurements.)

1. If you have the NEWSLETR keyboard, press **Ctrl-A**; otherwise press *Format* (**Shift-F8**), then choose **O**ther (4), **A**dvance (1)

   If you choose **L**eft (1), **R**ight (2), **U**p (1), or **D**own (2) from the menu, the words will be printed a distance relative to the cursor. If you choose **P**osition (6), the words will be placed a specific location measured from the left edge of the paper. If you choose L**i**ne (3), the words will be placed in a specific location measured from the top edge of the paper.

2. Choose L**i**ne (3)

    **NOTE:** Make sure that your **NumLock** key is on if you are using the numeric key pad to enter your numbers. Otherwise, WordPerfect thinks you are using arrow keys instead of number keys.

3. Type **11/12** and press **Enter**

   WordPerfect will calculate the decimal value (.917). You will not see the results of text placement at this time except on the status line when you return to the edit screen.

4. Choose **A**dvance (1)

5. Choose **P**osition (6)

6. Type **3 1/6** (or 3.17) and press **Enter**

7. Press *Exit* (**F7**) to exit the Format:Other menu and return to the Style (codes) screen

   Notice how WordPerfect converted fractions to decimals.

8. Type **Desktop Publishing** and press **Enter**

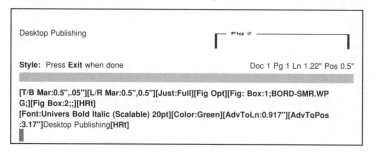

## Change the Color back to Black

1. Press *Font* (**Ctrl-F8**)

2. Choose Print **C**olor (5)

3. Choose Blac**k** (1)

4. Press *Exit* (**F7**) to exit the Print Color menu

## Position the Black Text "Desktop Publishing"

By looking at the other Advance codes, estimate the distance, slightly down and slightly to the left of the shadow. This distance can be edited after you have looked in *Print:View*.

1. If you have the NEWSLETR keyboard, press **Ctrl-A**; otherwise press *Format* (**Shift-F8**), then choose **O**ther (4), **A**dvance (1)

2. Choose L**i**ne (3)

3. Type **.95** and press **Enter**

   This will disappear from the screen, but will still create a code.

4. Choose **A**dvance (1)

5. Choose **P**osition (6)

6. Type **3.12** and press **Enter**

7. Press *Exit* (**F7**) to exit the Format:Other menu

8. Type **Desktop Publishing** and press **Enter** again

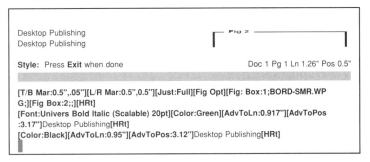

## Position Your Cursor for the Words "News Review"

1. If you have the NEWSLETR keyboard, press Ctrl-A; otherwise press *Format* (**Shift-F8**), then choose <u>O</u>ther (4), <u>A</u>dvance (1)

2. Choose <u>P</u>osition (6)

3. Type **2 1/5** (or 2.2) and press **Enter**

4. Press *Exit* (**F7**) to exit the Format:Other menu

## Change the Font for "News Review"

1. If you have the NEWSLETR keyboard, press **Ctrl-F**; otherwise press *Font* (**Ctrl-F8**) and choose <u>F</u>ont (4)

2. Move the cursor to CG Times Bold Italic (Scalable)

3. Choose <u>S</u>elect (1)

4. At Point size:, type **45** and press **Enter**

5. Type **News Review** and press **Enter**

```
Desktop Publishing                              ┌─ Fig 2 ─────────────────┐
Desktop Publishing                              │                         │
News Review                                     │                         │
Style: Press Exit when done                     └─────────────────────────┘
                                                    Doc 1 Pg 1 Ln 1.91" Pos 0.5"

[T/B Mar:0.5",.05"][L/R Mar:0.5",0.5"][Just:Full][Fig Opt][Fig: Box:1;BORD-SMR.WP
G;][Fig Box:2;;][HRt]
[Font:Univers Bold Italic (Scalable) 20pt][Color:Green][AdvToLn:0.917"][AdvToPos
:3.17"]Desktop Publishing[HRt]
[Color:Black][AdvToLn:0.95"][AdvToPos:3.12"]Desktop Publishing[HRt]
[AdvToPos:2.2"][Font:CG Times Bold Italic (Scalable) 45pt]News Review[HRt]
```

## Change the Font for the Dateline

1. If you have the NEWSLETR keyboard, press **Ctrl-F**;
   otherwise press *Font* (**Ctrl-F8**) and choose **F**ont (4)

2. Move the cursor to Univers (Scalable)

3. Choose **S**elect (1)

4. At Point size:, type **10** and press **Enter**

## Position the Dateline Down

1. Press **Enter** twice more for extra white space

   **NOTE:** You could also use the Advance to Line feature.

## Position the Dateline to the Left

1. If you have the NEWSLETR keyboard, press **Ctrl-A**;
   otherwise press *Format* (**Shift-F8**), then
   choose **O**ther (4), **A**dvance (1)

2. Choose **P**osition (6)

3. Type **1 2/5** and press **Enter**

4. Press *Exit* (**F7**) to exit the Format:Other menu

5. Type **January 1, 1993** (do *not* press **Enter**)

## Position the Words "Volume 1, Number 1"

1. If you have the NEWSLETR keyboard, press **Ctrl-A**;
   otherwise press *Format* (**Shift-F8**), then
   choose **O**ther (4), **A**dvance (1)

2. Choose **P**osition (6)

3. Type **4 4/5** and press **Enter**

4. Press *Exit* (**F7**) to exit the Format:Other menu

5. Type **Volume 1, Number 1** and press **Enter**

6. Press **Enter** three more times to position the headline

```
┌──────────────────────────────────────────────────────────────┐
│                                    ┌─ Fig 2 ──────────────┐    │
│  Desktop Publishing                │                      │    │
│  Desktop Publishing                │                      │    │
│  News Review                       │                      │    │
│                                                                │
│  January 1, 1993Volume 1,Number 1                              │
│                                                                │
│  Style:  press Exit when done            Doc 1 Pg 1 Ln 2.91" Pos 0.5" │
│  ▓▓▓▓▓▓▓▓▓▓▓▓▓▓▓▓▓▓▓▓▓▓▓▓▓▓▓▓▓▓▓▓▓▓▓▓▓▓▓▓▓▓▓▓▓▓▓▓▓▓▓▓▓▓        │
│  [T/B Mar:0.5",.05"][L/R Mar:0.5",0.5"][Just:Full][Fig Opt][Fig: Box:1;BORD-SMR.W │
│  PG;][Fig Box:2;;][HRt]                                         │
│  [Font:Univers Bold Italic (Scalable) 20pt][Color:Green][AdvToLn:0.917"][AdvToPos │
│  :3.17"]Desktop Publishing[HRt]                                 │
│  [Color:Black][AdvToLn:0.95"][AdvToPos:3.12"]Desktop Publishing[HRt] │
│  [AdvToPos:2.2"][Font:CG Times Bold Italic (Scalable) 45pt]News Review[HRt] │
│  [Font:Univers (Scalable) 10pt][HRt]                           │
│  [HRt]                                                          │
│  [AdvToPos:1.4"]January 1, 1993[AdvToPos:4.8"]Volume 1, Number 1[Hrt] │
│  [HRt]                                                          │
│  [HRt]                                                          │
│  [HRt]                                                          │
│  ▌                                                             │
└──────────────────────────────────────────────────────────────┘
```

## Exit Styles

1. Press *Exit* (**F7**) twice (once to exit the Styles (codes) screen and once to exit the Styles:Edit menu)

   Do *not* choose **O**n (1). Your masthead has already been placed in your editing screen.

2. Press *Exit* (**F7**) for the third time to exit the Styles menu

## Print View

1. If you have the NEWSLETR keyboard, press **Ctrl-P**; otherwise press *Print* (**Shift-F7**) and choose **V**iew (6)

   If you cannot see anything, choose Full Page (3) or choose 100% (1).

2. Press *Exit* (**F7**) when you have finished viewing your newsletter

Sometimes the location of your text is not quite where you would like it and you need to adjust the location. If you do *not* need to adjust your text, then jump to the section **Headline**.

## Edit and Add Codes to Masthead Style

1. Press *Style* (**Alt-F8**)
2. Highlight the Masthead style
3. Choose <u>E</u>dit (4)
4. Choose <u>C</u>odes (4)

## Adjust Any [Adv] Code

1. Place your cursor on the [AdvtoLn] or [AdvtoPos] code
2. Press **Ctrl-E** from the NEWSLETR keyboard (or **Alt-E** from the SHORTCUT keyboard) to edit the code
3. Choose either L<u>i</u>ne (3), <u>P</u>osition (6), or a direction (up, down, left or right)
4. Type your new measurement and press **Enter**
5. Press *Exit* to exit the Format:Other menu and return to the editing screen

# Headline

Press **Home**, **Home**, **Down Arrow** (↓) to position your cursor beyond all the codes. Use *Reveal Codes* (**F11**) to be sure your cursor is beyond your Masthead style. Sometimes *Print:View* will move your cursor.

Doc 1 Pg 1 Ln 2.91" Pos 0.5"

[Open Style:Masthead]

You created an open style for the masthead, meaning, in effect, that any formatting code you entered will be as if you had placed it in the document directly. In a paired style code, the codes surround the blocked text and are turned off again, leaving no effect on any text after the [Style Off] code.

## Create a Paired Style for the Headline

1. Press *Style* (**Alt-F8**)

2. Choose **C**reate (3)

3. Choose **N**ame (1)

4. Type **Headline** and press **Enter**

5. Choose **T**ype (2)

6. Choose **P**aired (1) (default)

7. Choose **D**escription (3)

8. Type **Universal, Bold, 25p, Center**, and press **Enter**

9. Choose **C**odes (4)

   **NOTE:** All codes should appear before the comment box.

## Select a Font, Center, and Turn on the Style

1. If you have the NEWSLETR keyboard, press **Ctrl-F**; otherwise press *Font* (**Ctrl-F8**) and choose **F**ont (4)

2. Move your cursor to Univers Bold (Scalable)

3. Choose **S**elect (1)

4. At Point size:, type **25** and press **Enter**

5. Choose *Center* (**Shift-F6**)

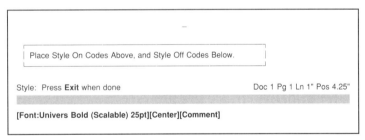

```
                              –

  ┌─────────────────────────────────────────────────────┐
  │ Place Style On Codes Above, and Style Off Codes Below. │
  └─────────────────────────────────────────────────────┘

  Style:  Press Exit when done                    Doc 1 Pg 1 Ln 1" Pos 4.25"

  [Font:Univers Bold (Scalable) 25pt][Center][Comment]
```

6. Press *Exit* (**F7**) to exit the Style (codes) screen

7. Press *Exit* (**F7**) to exit the Styles:Edit menu

   Do *not* choose **O**n (1). Later, you will place the headline inside a gray shaded text box.

8. Press *Exit* (**F7**) again to exit the Styles menu

## Set the Options for the Gray Shading Around the Headline "Welcome to Design"

1. Press *Graphics* (**Alt-F9**)

2. Choose Text **B**ox (3)

3. Choose **O**ptions (4)

4. Choose **B**order Style (1)

    Choose **N**one (1) four times

5. Choose **O**utside Border Space (2)

    Type **0** (zero) and press **Enter** (repeat four times)

6. Choose **I**nside Border Space (3)

    Type **.167** and press **Enter** (repeat four times)

7. Choose **G**ray Shading (% of black)

8. Type **10** and press **Enter** (default)

9. At Selection: <u>0</u>, press *Exit* (**F7**) to exit the Options:Text Box menu

## Create the Gray Shaded Text Box for the Headline "Welcome to Design"

1. Press *Graphics* (**Alt-F9**)

2. Choose Text **B**ox (3)

3. Choose **C**reate (1)

4. Choose **H**orizontal Position (6)

    Choose **R**ight (2)

5. Choose **S**ize (7)

    Choose Set **H**eight/Auto Width (2)

    Type **40p** (.556) and press **Enter**

The width, which automatically adjusts, is larger than the font size of 25 because you want a little gray above and below the text for aesthetics.

You will now add the style and the text in the Edit mode.

6. Choose Edit (9)

7. Press *Style* (**Alt-F8**)

8. Move your cursor to Headline

9. Choose On (1)

10. Type **Welcome to Design** between the [Style On:Headline] and [Style Off:Headline] codes; do *not* press **Enter**

11. Press *Exit* (**F7**) to exit the Edit mode and return to the Definition:Text Box menu

12. Press *Exit* (**F7**) to exit the Definition:Text Box menu

    You are now in the editing screen.

13. Press **Enter** twice

    You are now ready to create the rest of your newsletter.

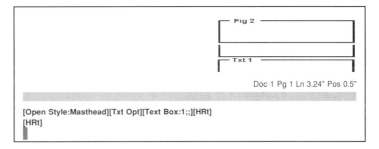

# Create Styles for Shortcuts

## Create a Paired Style for the Subheadings

1. Press *Style* (**Alt-F8**)

2. Choose Create (3)

3. Choose Name (1)

4. Type **Sub-Head** and press **Enter**

5. Choose Description (3)

6. Type **Universal, Bold, 14p, AdvDn .2** and press **Enter**

7. Choose **C**odes (4) to format the subhead

   You are now in the Style (codes) screen

   Instead of pressing **Enter** for a full line height, advance down for a partial line height so that everything will fit on one page.

8. If you have the NEWSLETR keyboard, press **Ctrl-A**; otherwise press *Format* (**Shift-F8**), then choose **O**ther (4), **A**dvance (1)

9. Choose **D**own (2)

10. Type **.2** and press **Enter**

11. Press *Exit* (**F7**) to exit the Format:Other menu

12. If you have the NEWSLETR keyboard, press **Ctrl-F**; otherwise press *Font* (**Ctrl-F8**) and choose **F**ont (4)

13. Move your cursor to Univers Bold (Scalable)

14. Choose **S**elect (1)

15. At Point size:, type **14** and press **Enter**

    You are now in the Style (codes) screen.

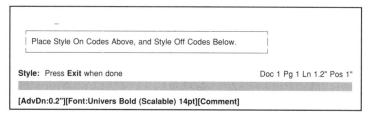

16. Press *Exit* (**F7**) to exit the Style (codes) screen

17. Press *Exit* (**F7**) to exit the Styles:Edit menu

    You will not use this style at the moment.

## Create an Open Style for Regular Text

1. While still in the Styles menu, choose **C**reate (3)

2. Choose **N**ame (1)

3. Type **Regular Text** and press **Enter**

4. Choose **T**ype (2)

5. Choose **O**pen (2)

 **NOTE:** Because this is an open style, you no longer have option (5), which deals with how to get out of a paired style, on the menu.

6. Choose **D**escription (3)

7. Type **CG Times, 12p** and press **Enter**

8. Choose **C**odes (4) to format the text

9. If you have the NEWSLETR keyboard, press **Ctrl-F**; otherwise press *Font* (**Ctrl-F8**) and choose **F**ont (4)

10. Move the cursor to CG Times (Scalable)

11. Choose **S**elect (1)

12. At Point size:, type **12** and press **Enter**

13. Press *Exit* (**F7**) to exit the Style (codes) screen

14. Press *Exit* (**F7**) to exit the Styles:Edit menu

15. Press *Exit* (**F7**) to exit the Styles menu and return to the editing screen without selecting a style

# Clarity!

## Set the Position Before Typing the First Subhead "Clarity!"

1. If you have the NEWSLETR keyboard, press **Ctrl-A**; otherwise press *Format* (**Shift-F8**), then choose **O**ther (4), **A**dvance (1)

2. Choose **P**osition (6)

3. Type **1.5** and press **Enter**

4. Press *Exit* (**F7**) to exit the Format:Other menu

## Use Sub-Head Style for the Subhead "Clarity!"

1. Press *Style* (**Alt-F8**)

2. Move the cursor to Sub-Head style

3. Choose **O**n (1)

4. Type **Clarity!** between the [Style On] and [Style Off] codes; then press **Right Arrow** (→) to move out of the Sub-Head style codes

   Your cursor, which was on [Style Off:Sub-Head], should now be beyond the [Style Off:Sub-Head] code.

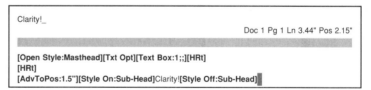

```
Clarity!_
                                                    Doc 1 Pg 1 Ln 3.44" Pos 2.15"

[Open Style:Masthead][Txt Opt][Text Box:1;;][HRt]
[HRt]
[AdvToPos:1.5"][Style On:Sub-Head]Clarity![Style Off:Sub-Head]
```

## Use the Regular Text Style

1. Press *Style* (**Alt-F8**)

2. Move the cursor to Regular Text style

3. Choose **O**n (1)

4. Press **Enter** to go to the next line

# Balance

## Set the Text Box Options for "Balance"

1. Press *Graphics* (**Alt-F9**)

2. Choose Text **B**ox (3)

3. Choose **O**ptions (4)

4. Choose **B**order Style (1)

    Choose **S**ingle (2) four times

5. Choose **O**utside Border Space (2)

    Type **.167** and press **Enter** (repeat four times)

6. Choose **I**nside Border Space (3)

    Type **.1** and press **Enter** (repeat four times)

7. Choose **G**ray Shading (% of black) (9)

    Type **10** and press **Enter** (default)

8. At Selection: **0**, press *Exit* (**F7**) when done

## Create the Text Box for "Balance"

1. Press *Graphics* (**Alt-F9**)

2. Choose Text **B**ox (3)

3. Choose **C**reate (3)

4. Set Anchor **t**ype (4) to **P**aragraph (1) (default)

5. Set **V**ertical Position (5) to **0** (default)

6. Set **H**orizontal Position (6) to **R**ight (2) (default)

7. Choose **S**ize (7)

    Choose Set **W**idth/Auto Height (1)

    Type **2** and press **Enter** (the height is automatically adjusted)

## Add Text to the Text Box

1. Choose Edit (9)

2. Press *Center* (**Shift-F6**)

3. If you have the NEWSLETR keyboard, press **Ctrl-F**; otherwise press *Font* (**Ctrl-F8**) and choose Font (4)

4. Move your cursor to Univers Bold (Scalable)

5. Choose Select (1)

6. At Point size:, type **13** and press **Enter**

7. Type **Balance** (the title)

8. Press **Enter** twice (once to end the line and once to create a blank line)

9. If you have the NEWSLETR keyboard, press **Ctrl-F**; otherwise press *Font* (**Ctrl-F8**) and choose Font (4)

10. Move the cursor to CG Times (Scalable)

11. Choose Select (1)

12. At Point size:, type **10** and press **Enter**

13. Type your text

    **NOTE:** Do not press **Enter** on the last line unless you want more white space at the end than allocated in the previously set Text Box options.

14 Press *Exit* (**F7**) to exit the Box: screen

15. Press *Exit* (**F7**) to exit the Definition:Text Box menu

# Drop Cap

## Create an Open Style for the Drop Cap

1. Press *Style* (**Alt-F8**)
2. Choose **C**reate (3)
3. Choose **N**ame (1) to type a style name
4. Type **Drop Cap** and press **Enter**
5. Choose **T**ype (2), then choose **O**pen (2)
6. Choose **D**escription (3)
7. Type **CG Times, 60p** and press **Enter**
8. Choose **C**odes (4) to format the text

## Create Figure Options with No Border and Zero Inside and Outside Space

1. Press *Graphics* (**Alt-F9**)
2. Choose **F**igure (1)
3. Choose **O**ptions (4)
4. Choose **B**order Style (1)

   Choose **N**one (1) four times
5. Choose **O**utside Border Space (2)

   Type **0** (zero) and press **Enter** (repeat four times)
6. Choose **I**nside Border Space (3)

   Type **0** (zero) and press **Enter** (repeat four times)
7. Press *Exit* (**F7**) to exit the Options:Figure menu

   You will now be at the Style (codes) screen

## Create the Box to Hold the Drop Cap "C"

1. Press **Ctrl-G** from either soft keyboard

    **NOTE:** This the same as pressing *Graphics* (**Alt-F9**), then choosing **F**igure (1), **C**reate (1)

2. Set Anchor **T**ype (4) to **P**aragraph (1) (default)

    **NOTE:** This is not a character type even though you will be inserting a character inside the box. A character type only allows one line of text next to it unless you make several adjustments.

3. Set **H**orizontal Position (6) to **L**eft (1)

4. Choose **S**ize (7)

   Choose Set **B**oth (3)

   For width, type **45p** (.625) and press **Enter**

   For height, type **50p** (.694) and press **Enter** (this is a little more than three lines of regular text)

5. Choose **E**dit (9)

6. If you have the NEWSLETR keyboard, press **Ctrl-F**; otherwise press *Font* (**Ctrl-F8**) and choose **F**ont (4)

7. Move the cursor to CG Times Bold (Scalable)

8. Choose **S**elect (1)

9. At Point size:, type **60** and press **Enter**

10. Type **C** (do not press **Enter**)

11. Press *Exit* (**F7**) to exit the Box: screen

12. Press *Exit* (**F7**) to exit the Definition:Figure menu

    The font for the character is larger than the box because the point size of a character is measured from the tallest capital letter to the lowest descending letter. The letter **C** doesn't descend. If you use *Print:View* and the letter does not show, the font is too large. It takes trial and error to become familiar with your fonts.

13. Press *Exit* (**F7**) to exit the Style (codes) screen

14. Press *Exit* (**F7**) to exit the Styles:Edit menu

15. Choose **O**n (1) to turn on the style

# Advance the Regular Text Down

There should be only three lines of regular text next to the letter, and the letter should stand a little higher than the first line of text.

1. If you have the NEWSLETR keyboard, press **Ctrl-A**; otherwise press *Format* (**Shift-F8**), then choose **O**ther (4), **A**dvance (1)

2. Choose **D**own (2)

3. Type **10p** (.139) and press **Enter**

   **NOTE:** This is not quite the height of a line of regular text; through trial and error you will learn where to advance text and graphics.

4. Press *Exit* (**F7**) to exit the Format:Other menu

## Type the Text

When done, press **Enter** twice (once to end the paragraph and once to create a blank line).

# Consistency!

## Set the Position Before Typing the Subhead "Consistency!"

1. If you have the NEWSLETR keyboard, press **Ctrl-A**; otherwise press *Format* (**Shift-F8**), then choose **O**ther (4), **A**dvance (1).

2. Choose **P**osition (6)

3. Type **2.6** and press **Enter**

4. Press *Exit* (**F7**) to exit the Format:Other menu

## Use Sub-Head Style for the Next Subhead "Consistency!"

1. Press *Style* (**Alt-F8**)

2. Press **PgDn** key to move the cursor to Sub-Head style

3. Choose **O**n (1)

4. Type **Consistency!** then press the **Right Arrow** (→) to move out of the Sub-Head style code

   Your cursor was on [Style Off:Sub-head]; now it should be beyond the [Style Off:Sub-Head] code.

5. Press **Enter** twice (once to go to the next line and once to create a blank line)

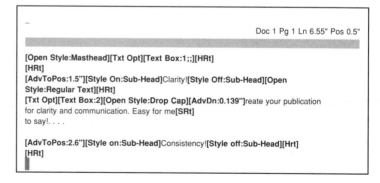

```
 ⁻
                                              Doc 1 Pg 1 Ln 6.55" Pos 0.5"

[Open Style:Masthead][Txt Opt][Text Box:1;;][HRt]
[HRt]
[AdvToPos:1.5"][Style On:Sub-Head]Clarity![Style Off:Sub-Head][Open
Style:Regular Text][HRt]
[Txt Opt][Text Box:2][Open Style:Drop Cap][AdvDn:0.139"]reate your publication
for clarity and communication. Easy for me[SRt]
to say!. . . .

[AdvToPos:2.6"][Style on:Sub-Head]Consistency![Style off:Sub-Head][Hrt]
[HRt]
```

## Type Your Text

When done, press **Enter** twice.

# Experiment!

## Set the Position Before Typing the Subhead "Experiment!"

1. If you have the NEWSLETR keyboard, press **Ctrl-A**; otherwise press *Format* (**Shift-F8**), then choose Other (4), Advance (1)

2. Choose Position (6)

3. Type **4.38** and press **Enter**

4. Press *Exit* (**F7**) to exit the Format:Other menu

## Use Sub-Head Style for the Next Subhead "Experiment!"

1. Press *Style* (**Alt-F8**)

2. Press **PgDn** key to move the cursor to Sub-Head style

3. Choose On (1)

4. Type **Experiment!** between the [Style On] and [Style Off] codes; then press the **Right Arrow** (→) to move out of the Sub-Head style code

   Your cursor was on [Style Off:Sub-Head]; now it should be beyond the [Style Off:Sub-Head] code.

5. Press **Enter** twice (once to go to the next line and once to create a blank line)

```
  –
                                                      Doc 1 Pg 1 Ln 8.34" Pos 0.5"


[Open Style:Masthead][Txt Opt][Text Box:1;;][HRt]
[HRt]
[AdvToPos.1.5"][Style On:Sub-Head]Clarity![Style Off:Sub-Head][Open
Style:Regular Text][HRt]
[Txt Opt][Text Box:2][Open Style:Drop Cap][AdvDn:0.139"]reate your publication
for clarity and communication. Easy for me[SRt]
to say!. . . .


[AdvToPos:2.6"][Style on:Sub-Head]Consistency![Style off:Sub-Head][Hrt]
Being consistent . . . . .


[AdvToPos:4.38"][Style on:Sub-Head]Experiment![Style off:Sub-Head][Hrt]
```

# Add a Graphic Image with a Caption

## Create Your Figure Options with No Border

1. Press *Graphics* (**Alt-F9**)

2. Choose **F**igure (1)

3. Choose **O**ptions (4)

4. Choose **B**order Style (1)

    Choose **N**one (1) four times

5. Choose **O**utside Border Space (2)

    Left: Type **0** (zero) and press **Enter**

    Right: Type **.167** and press **Enter**

    Top: Type **.167** and press **Enter**

    Bottom: Type **0** (zero) and press **Enter**

6. Choose **I**nside Border Space (3)

    Type **0** (zero) and press **Enter** (repeat four times)

7. Choose **P**osition of Caption (7)

    Choose **B**elow Box (1)

    Choose **O**utside of Border (1)

8. Press *Exit* (**F7**) to exit the Options:Figure menu

## Add the Graphic

The graphic will be horizontally positioned to the left.

1. Press **Ctrl-G** for Graphics from either soft keyboard

   **NOTE:** This the same as pressing *Graphics* (**Alt-F9**), then choosing **F**igure (1), **C**reate (1)

2. Choose **F**ilename (1)

3. Press *List* (**F5**), **Enter**

4. Highlight the picture you want

   My example was: C:\WIN31\LAYOUT.PCX; however, you can use any .WPG, .TIF, or other graphic that is compatible with WordPerfect.

   **NOTE:** The thumbnail sketches in the example were created in a paint program, saved as a .PCX file, and then retrieved into a WordPerfect graphics box in the usual way.

5. Choose **R**etrieve (1)

6. Choose **H**orizontal Position (6)

   Choose **L**eft (1)

7. Choose **S**ize (7)

   Choose Set **H**eight/Auto Width (2)

   Type **1.5** and press **Enter** for the height

   The width is automatically adjusted.

## The Caption

1. Choose **C**aption (3)

2. Press **Backspace** to remove the figure number

3. If you have the NEWSLETR keyboard, press **Ctrl-F**; otherwise press *Font* (**Ctrl-F8**) and choose **F**ont (4)

4. Move your cursor to Univers Bold (Scalable)

5. Choose **S**elect (1)

6. At Point size:, type **9** and press **Enter**

7. Press *Center* (**Shift-F6**)

8.  Type **These are thumbnail sketches** (the first line of text) and press **Enter**

9.  Press *Center* (**Shift-F6**)

10. Type **with facing pages (Spread).** (the second line of text); do *not* press **Enter**

11. Press *Exit* (**F7**) to exit the Box Caption: screen

12  Press *Exit* (**F7**) to exit the Definition:Figure menu

13. Press **Enter** to go to the next line

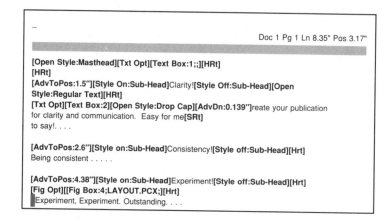

## Type the Rest of the Text

# Make Adjustments

If all of the text does not fit or if you have too much space at the bottom of the page

*   Find the distance to adjust
*   Press *Style* (**Alt-F8**) to edit your subhead style and use the Advance feature. If you have the NEWSLETR keyboard, press **Ctrl-A**; otherwise press *Format* (**Shift-F8**), **O**ther (4), **A**dvance (1), to add or subtract white space where it will not be noticed.
*   Change the size of the regular text font in the styles
*   Adjust the font size of your headline in styles

# Final Look

## A Final Look Before Printing

1. If you have the NEWSLETR keyboard, press **Ctrl-P**; otherwise press *Print* (**Shift-F7**) and choose **V**iew (6)

2. Choose **F**ull Page (3)

3. When you are ready to print, press *Cancel* (**F1**) to return to the Print menu

4. Choose **F**ull Document (1)

## Save Your Newsletter Styles in a File

1. Press *Style* (**Alt-F8**)

2. Choose **S**ave (6)

3. Type **WELCOME.STY** and press **Enter**

4. Press *Exit* (**F7**) to exit the Styles menu

## Return to WordPerfect's Original Soft Keyboard

1. Press *Setup* (**Shift-F1**)

2. Choose **K**eyboard (5)

3. Choose **O**riginal (6)

4. Press *Exit* (**F7**) to exit the Setup menu

## Save Your Document

*Desktop Publishing*
**News Review**

January 1, 1993
Volume 1, Number 1

# Linking Your Spreadsheet and Graphs
# What a Breeze !!

## Create Your Spreadsheet & Graph

Use your normal spreadsheet program and create your spreadsheet as usual. Keep in mind the width of your

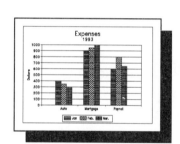

spreadsheet. It must fit on one sheet of paper or WordPerfect will squish it beyond recognition.

Create your graph in your spreadsheet program. When you are finished, save it as a *.PIC file in the directory where you normally store your **WordPerfect** graphics.

(C:\WP51\GRAPHICS)

## Retrieve and Link in WordPerfect

Use WordPerfect to move your cursor where you would like your graph to appear. Press **Alt-F9**

(graphics key) and set the frame option you like. Press **Alt-F9** again, box style, then create. First select Contents to tell WordPerfect the information is coming from the disk. Then select filename.PIC.

You want the information to come from the disk instead of from a regular graphics file so that when you update the spreadsheet in your spreadsheet program and then resave your graph, your graph will also be updated automatically in WordPerfect. Otherwise, if you had retrieved it as a regular graphics file, you would have to retrieve it again and again.

## Table Placement

A WordPerfect table cannot be placed in a column in column mode as a table. You must insert it in a graphics box.

First switch documents, link your spreadsheet using **Ctrl-F5**, and make all necessary changes. Block and move the table into a graphics box; any one will do. Then place the graphics box in the column.

To make a graphics box span two columns, create the box before you turn the column mode on, then tell WordPerfect it is a page type and where to place it.

| Expenses | | | | |
|---|---|---|---|---|
| | Jan | Feb. | Mar. | 1st-Qtr. Totals |
| Auto | 400 | 350 | 300 | 1050 |
| Mortgage | 900 | 950 | 1000 | 2850 |
| Payroll | 600 | 800 | 650 | 2050 |
| Total | 1900 | 2100 | 1950 | 5950 |

# 4

# Linking Your Spreadsheet: The Keystrokes

## Getting Started

Every newsletter has a different format. Some look better than others because of their creator's experience. To gain proficiency, you will now create a style sheet for the masthead. But first make sure you do not have a default style library.

Start with an empty edit screen.

### Removing a Default Library

1. Press *Setup* (**Shift-F1**)

2. Choose **L**ocation of files (6)

3. Choose **S**tyle Files (5)

4. Press **Enter** on the style directory

5. Delete any style name that appears on the second line

6. Then press **Enter**

7. Press *Exit* (**F7**) to return to your document

### Clear the Current Style Library of All Old Styles

1. Press *Style* (**Alt-F8**)

   If there are no styles, press *Exit* (**F7**) and move to **Use your NEWSLETR Keyboard...**

2. Position the cursor on the style to be deleted

3. Choose **D**elete (5)

4. Choose **D**efinition Only (3)

5. Delete all style names you do not want

6. Press *Exit* (**F7**) when you are finished

### Select a Soft Keyboard

If you did not create the soft keyboard called NEWSLETR, either return to Lesson 1 and create it or select the SHORTCUT keyboard that came with WordPerfect.

1. Press *Setup* (**Shift-F1**)

2. Choose **K**eyboard (5)

3. Move your cursor to NEWSLETR (preferably) or SHORTCUT

4. Choose **S**elect (1)

5. Press *Exit* (**F7**)

# Create the Masthead Style

### Create an Open Style

1. Press *Style* (**Alt-F8**)

2. Choose **C**reate (3)

3. Choose **N**ame (1)

4. Type **Masthead** and press **Enter**

5. Choose <u>T</u>ype (2)

6. Choose <u>O</u>pen (2)

7. Choose <u>D</u>escription (3)

8. Type **Graphic w/Shadow text, Dateline with Shaded lines** and press **Enter**

9. Choose <u>C</u>odes (4) to format the Masthead style

    You should be in the Style (codes) screen.

**Style:** Press **Exit** when done        Doc 1 Pg 1 Ln 1" Pos 1"

## Set the Margins ½" All Around

1. Press *Format* (**Shift-F8**)

2. Choose <u>P</u>age (2)

    You should be at the Format:Page menu.

3. Choose <u>M</u>argins (5)

4. Type **.5** and press **Enter**

5. Type **1/2** and press **Enter**

    **NOTE:** You can use either decimals or fractions when you enter a unit of measure.

6. At Selection: <u>0</u>, press **Enter** to exit the Format:Page screen and return to the Format screen

    **NOTE:** If you press *Exit* (**F7**), you will return to your document. By pressing **Enter**, you go only one menu level backward. If you pressed *Exit* (**F7**) by mistake and are now in the edit screen, press *Format* (**Shift-F8**) to get back on track.

7. Choose <u>L</u>ine (1)

    You should be at the Format:Line menu.

8. Choose **M**argins (7)

9. Type **.5** and press **Enter**

10. Type **.5** and press **Enter**

11. Choose **J**ustification (3)

12. Choose **L**eft (1)

13. Press *Exit* (**F7**) to exit all format menus

   You will now be in the Style (codes) screen.

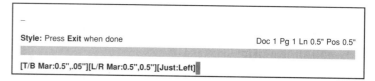

## Set the Options for the Graphic Border

1. Press *Graphics* (**Alt-F9**)

2. Choose **F**igure (1)

3. Choose **O**ptions (4)

4. Choose **B**order Style (1)

   Type **N** for none four times

5. Choose **O**utside Border Space (2)

   Type **0** (zero) and press **Enter** (repeat four times)

6. Choose **I**nside Border Space (3)

   Type **0** (zero) and press **Enter** (repeat four times)

   Your cursor should now be at Selection: <u>0</u>

7. Press *Exit* (**F7**) to exit the Options:Figure menu

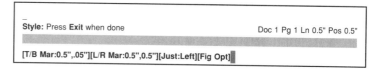

## Add the Graphic

Make sure your cursor is beyond the [Fig Opt] code. The options must be first or the graphic will not know about them.

1. Press **Ctrl-G** from either soft keyboard

    **NOTE:** This the same as pressing *Graphics* (**Alt-F9**), then choosing **F**igure (1), **C**reate (1)

   You should be at the Definition:Figure menu.

2. Choose C**o**ntents (2)

3. Choose Graphic on **D**isk (2)

   There are two ways to insert graphics into a document. One is to retrieve a graphic and have it become a part of your document. The other is to tell WordPerfect where the graphic is so that, when it comes time to print the graphic, WordPerfect will print the graphic from the disk. Your document takes less disk space with this style of inserting graphics, but you must not remove your graphic or move it to another location; if you do WordPerfect will not be able to print it

    **NOTE:** The graphic must remain on the disk because style sheets cannot hold graphics. Tell WordPerfect that the graphic will remain on the disk before acknowledging which graphic you want.

4. Choose **F**ilename (1)

5. Choose *List* (**F5**) and press **Enter**

6. Highlight the picture you want
      For example, DOLLAR.WPG

7. Choose **R**etrieve (1)

   You should be at the Definition:Figure menu.

8. Choose **H**orizontal Position (6)

      Choose **L**eft (1)

9. Choose **S**ize (7)

> Choose Set **H**eight/Auto Width (2)
>
> Type **1.5** and press **Enter**

When you set the **H**eight (2), the width is automatically adjusted. The height of the graphic is the height of your fonts plus a little more (36p + 72p = 1.5"). Your fonts are 25p + 50p + leading (above, between, and below the headline text).

**NOTE:** There are approximately 72 points to 1 inch. A point is measured from the tallest capital letter to the lowest descending letter, for example: Ty.

10. At Selection: <u>0</u>, press *Exit* (**F7**) to exit the Definition:Figure menu and return to the Style (codes) screen

11. Press **Enter** so the text and graphic are not on the same line

You will now see a partial box labelled "Fig. 1." To keep the computer's response time as fast as possible, WordPerfect does not draw the image. You can, however, see it in *Print:View* mode.

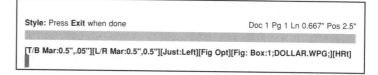

**Style:** Press **Exit** when done                     Doc 1 Pg 1 Ln 0.667" Pos 2.5"

[T/B Mar:0.5",.05"][L/R Mar:0.5",0.5"][Just:Left][Fig Opt][Fig: Box:1;DOLLAR.WPG;][HRt]

# Check Your Work

At any time, you can exit the Masthead style, look at the results in *Print:View*, and then return to the style where you left off. The following instructions describe how to do this.

## Exit Styles

1. Press *Exit* (**F7**) twice (once to exit the Styles (codes) screen and once to exit the Styles:Edit menu)

2. Choose <u>O</u>n (1) to place the masthead on your paper

   **NOTE:** Choose <u>O</u>n just once, no matter how many times you go in and out of your style to edit it. If you press <u>O</u>n more than once, you will have the masthead in your document more than once. If that happens, delete the second style code from your editing screen.

   You are now at your editing screen.

## Print View

1. Press *Print* (**Shift-F7**)

2. Choose <u>V</u>iew (6)

3. Press *Exit* (**F7**) to return to your editing screen

## Edit and Add Codes to Masthead Style

1. Press *Style* (**Alt-F8**)

2. Highlight the Masthead style

3. Choose <u>E</u>dit (4)

4. Choose <u>C</u>odes (4)

5. Press **Home**, **Home**, **Down Arrow** (↓) to position your cursor beyond the codes

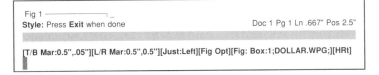

71

# Set the Words "Desktop Publishing"

## Select Font for the Words "Desktop Publishing"

1. If you have the NEWSLETR keyboard, press **Ctrl-F**; otherwise press *Font* (**Ctrl-F8**) and choose **F**ont (4)

2. Move the cursor to Univers Bold Italic (Scalable)

3. Choose **S**elect (1)

4. At Point size:, type **25** and press **Enter**

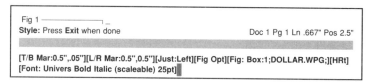

## Establish a Position for the Words "Desktop Publishing"

WordPerfect's Advance feature allows you to place text anywhere on your paper regardless of cursor location. (You might want to use your ruler for your measurements.)

To use the Advance Code, apply the following rules:

- If you choose **L**eft (4), **R**ight (2), **U**p (1) or **D**own (2) from the menu, the words will be printed a distance *relative* to the cursor.
- If you choose **P**osition (6), the words will be placed at a specific location measured from the left edge of the paper. This has no relationship to the cursor or the text.
- If you choose L**i**ne (3), the words will be placed in a specific location measured from the top edge of the paper. This has no relationship to the cursor or the text.

1. Press *Format* (**Shift-F8**)

2. Choose **O**ther (4)

3. Choose **A**dvance (1)

4. Choose L**i**ne (3)

5. Type **.705** and press **Enter**

   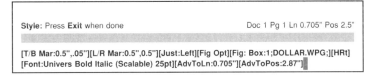

   **NOTE:** I pressed **Enter** first to accept WordPerfect's default cursor location. After viewing, I readjusted the line location down a little, to .705, as shown below.

6. Choose **A**dvance (1)

7. Choose **P**osition (6)

8. Type **2.87** and press **Enter**

   This is the default plus 1 character (the previous cursor location plus 25p).

9. At Selection: 0, press *Exit* (**F7**) to exit the Format:Other menu

---

**Style:** Press **Exit** when done        Doc 1 Pg 1 Ln 0.705" Pos 2.5"

[T/B Mar:0.5",.05"][L/R Mar:0.5",0.5"][Just:Left][Fig Opt][Fig: Box:1;DOLLAR.WPG;][HRt]
[Font:Univers Bold Italic (Scalable) 25pt][AdvToLn:0.705"][AdvToPos:2.87"]

---

## Type Your Masthead Text

1. Type **Desktop Publishing** and press **Enter**

## Exit Styles

1. Press *Exit* (**F7**) twice (once to exit the Styles (codes) screen and once to exit the Styles:Edit menu)

   Do *not* choose **O**n (1). Your masthead has already been placed in your editing screen.

2. Press *Exit* (**F7**) again to exit the Styles menu

## Print View

1. Press *Print* (**Shift-F7**)

2. Choose <u>V</u>iew (6)

3. Press *Exit* (**F7**) when you have finished

## Edit and Add Codes to Masthead Style

1. Press *Style* (**Alt-F8**)

2. Highlight the Masthead style

3. Choose <u>E</u>dit (4)

4. Choose <u>C</u>odes (4)

5. Press **Home**, **Home**, **Down Arrow** (↓) to position your cursor beyond all the codes

```
Style: Press Exit when done                          Doc 1 Pg 1 Ln 1.08" Pos 2.5"


[T/B Mar:0.5",.05"][L/R Mar:0.5",0.5"][Just:Left][Fig Opt][Fig: Box:1;DOLLAR.WPG;][HRt]
[Font:Univers Bold Italic (Scalable) 25pt][AdvToLn:0.705"][AdvToPos:2.87"] Deskto
p Publishing[HRt]
```

## Adjust Any [Adv] Code

Sometimes your text is not quite where you would like it and you need to adjust the location. If you don't need to adjust your text, move to **The Words "News Review."**

1. Place your cursor on the [AdvtoLn] or [AdvtoPos] code

2. Press **Ctrl-E** (from the NEWSLETR keyboard) or **Alt-E** (from the SHORTCUT keyboard) to edit the code

3. Choose either <u>L</u>ine (3), <u>P</u>osition (6), or a direction (up, down, left, or right)

4. Type your new measurement and press **Enter**

# Set the Words "News Review"

## Select a Font for "News Review"

1. If you have the NEWSLETR keyboard, press **Ctrl-F**; otherwise press *Font* (**Ctrl-F8**) and choose <u>F</u>ont (4)

2. Move the cursor to Univers Bold Italic (Scalable)

3. Choose <u>S</u>elect (1)

4. At Point size:, type **50** and press **Enter**

---

**Style:** Press **Exit** when done          Doc 1 Pg 1 Ln 1.08" Pos 2.5"

[T/B Mar:0.5",.05"][L/R Mar:0.5",0.5"][Left:Just][Fig Opt][Fig: Box:1;DOLLAR.WPG;][HRt]
[Font:Univers Bold Italic (Scalable) 25pt][AdvToLn:0.705"][AdvToPos:2.87"] Deskto
p Publishing[HRt]
[Font:Univers Bold Italic (Scalable) 50pt]

---

## Create the Shading for "News Review"

The shadow effect only works with printers that use PCL-5 language—the HP LaserJet III, IV, or compatibles. You can also use a soft font program that is compatible with the PCL-5 printer language. If you choose a color other than black, each color will print in a different shade of gray.

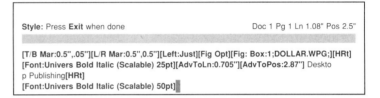

1. Press *Font* (**Ctrl-F8**)

2. Choose Print **C**olor (5)

   Notice the 0 (zero) percentages for black at the current color line.

3. Choose **G**reen (4)

   See how the percentages at the color line have changed.

4. Press *Exit* (**F7**) to exit the Print:Color Menu screen

---

**Style:** Press **Exit** when done        Doc 1 Pg 1 Ln 1.08" Pos 2.5"

[T/B Mar:0.5",.05"][L/R Mar:0.5",0.5"][Just:Left][Fig Opt][Fig: Box:1;DOLLAR.WPG;][HRt]
[Font:Univers Bold Italic (Scalable) 25pt][AdvToLn:0.705"][AdvToPos:2.87"] Deskto
p Publishing[HRt]
[Font:Univers Bold Italic (Scalable) 50pt][Color:Green]

---

## Establish a Position for the Shadow Print of "News Review"

1. Press *Format* (**Shift-F8**)

2. Choose **O**ther (4)

3. Choose **A**dvance (1)

4. Choose L**i**ne (3)

5. Type **1.1** and press **Enter**

6. Choose **A**dvance (1)

7. Choose **P**osition (6)

8. Type **2.97** and press **Enter**

   This is slightly to the right of where the black text "News Review" will print.

9. Press *Exit* (**F7**) to exit the Format:Other menu and return to the Style screen

 **NOTE:** When using color (shading), note the location of your cursor on the status line and write it down (line and position), then use the Format:Advance feature to place the second (black) text slightly lower and to the left.

---

**Style:** Press **Exit** when done                                    Doc 1 Pg 1 Ln 1.1" Pos 2.97"

[T/B Mar:0.5",.05"][L/R Mar:0.5",0.5"][Just:Left][Fig Opt][Fig: Box:1;DOLLAR.WPG;][HRt]
[Font:Univers Bold Italic (Scalable) 25pt][AdvToLn:0.705"][AdvToPos:2.87"] Deskto
p Publishing[HRt]
[Font:Univers Bold Italic (Scalable) 50pt][Color:Green][AdvToLn:1.1"][AdvToPos:2
.97"]

---

## Type Your Masthead Text

1. Write down the line and position shown on your status line (Ln = 1.1" and Pos = 2.97").

2. Type **News Review** and press **Enter**

## Change the Color back to Black

1. Press *Font* (**Ctrl-F8**)

2. Choose Print **C**olor (5)

3. Choose Blac**k** (1)

4. Press *Exit* (**F7**) to exit the Print Color screen

---

**Style:** Press **Exit** when done                                    Doc 1 Pg 1 Ln 1.82" Pos 2.5"

[T/B Mar:0.5",.05"][L/R Mar:0.5",0.5"][Just:Left][Fig Opt][Fig: Box:1;DOLLAR.WPG;][HRt]
[Font:Univers Bold Italic (Scalable) 25pt][AdvToLn:0.705"][AdvToPos:2.87"] Deskto
p Publishing[HRt]
[Font:Univers Bold Italic (Scalable) 50pt][Color:Green][AdvToLn:1.1"][AdvToPos:2
.97"]News Review[HRt]
[Color:Black]

---

## Position the Text

Now let's position the black text slightly down and to the left of the shadow.

1. Press *Format* (**Shift-F8**)
2. Choose **O**ther (4)
3. Choose **A**dvance (1)
4. Choose L**i**ne (3)
5. Type **1.2** and press **Enter**
6. Choose **A**dvance (1)
7. Choose **P**osition (6)
8. Type **2.87** and press **Enter**
9. At Selection: <u>0</u>, press *Exit* (**F7**) to exit the Format:Other menu
10. Type **News Review** again

# Set The Dateline

## Change Font Size for the Dateline

After "News Review," change the font before pressing **Enter**. The line height of **Enter** is based on the font size, and a large amount of white space between lines is unattractive.

1. If you have the NEWSLETR keyboard, press **Ctrl-F**; otherwise press *Font* (**Ctrl-F8**) and choose **F**ont (4)
2. Move your cursor to Univers (Scalable)
3. Choose **S**elect (1)
4. At Point size:, type **10** and press **Enter**
5. Press **Enter** twice more to position the cursor

Style: Press **Exit** when done                    Doc 1 Pg 1 Ln 2.09" Pos 0.5"

[T/B Mar:0.5",.05"][L/R Mar:0.5",0.5"][Just:Left][Fig Opt][Fig: Box:1;DOLLAR.WPG;][HRt]
[Font:Univers Bold Italic (Scalable) 25pt][AdvToLn:0.705"][AdvToPos:2.87"] Deskto
p Publishing[HRt]
[Font:Univers Bold Italic (Scalable) 50pt][Color:Green][AdvToLn:1.1"][AdvToPos:2
.97"]News Review[HRt]
[Color:Black][AdvToLn:1.2"][AdvToPos:2.87"]News Review[Font:Univers (Scalable) 1
0pt][HRt]
[HRt]

# Create Shaded Lines Surrounding the Dateline

Thirteen horizontal lines of varying shades of gray and thicknesses create a shaded effect.

## First Line (Ln = 2.09")

1. Press *Graphics* (**Alt-F9**)

2. Choose **L**ine (5)

   There are two horizontal lines and two vertical lines to choose from. One set is for creating a line; the other is for editing a previously created line.

3. Choose **H**orizontal (1)

4. Press *Exit* (**F7**) to exit the Graphics:Horizontal Line menu

   Pressing *Exit* retains the standard black hairline defaults.

5. Press **Enter** to go to the next line

   This line will not show on the edit screen except as a code in Reveal Codes.

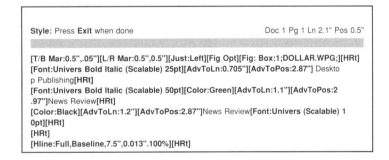

Style: Press **Exit** when done                    Doc 1 Pg 1 Ln 2.1" Pos 0.5"

[T/B Mar:0.5",.05"][L/R Mar:0.5",0.5"][Just:Left][Fig Opt][Fig: Box:1;DOLLAR.WPG;][HRt]
[Font:Univers Bold Italic (Scalable) 25pt][AdvToLn:0.705"][AdvToPos:2.87"] Deskto
p Publishing[HRt]
[Font:Univers Bold Italic (Scalable) 50pt][Color:Green][AdvToLn:1.1"][AdvToPos:2
.97"]News Review[HRt]
[Color:Black][AdvToLn:1.2"][AdvToPos:2.87"]News Review[Font:Univers (Scalable) 1
0pt][HRt]
[HRt]
[Hline:Full,Baseline,7.5",0.013".100%][HRt]

79

### Second Line (Ln = 2.1")

1. Press *Graphics* (**Alt-F9**)
2. Choose **L**ine (5)
3. Choose **H**orizontal (1)
4. Choose **W**idth (4)
5. Type **.03** and press **Enter**
6. Choose **G**ray Shading (5)
7. Type **70** and press **Enter**

   This is dark gray, or 70% black.

8. Press *Exit* (**F7**) to exit the Graphics:Horizontal Line menu
9. Press **Enter** to go to the next line

### Third Line (Ln = 2.13")

1. Press *Graphics* (**Alt-F9**)
2. Choose **L**ine (5)
3. Choose **H**orizontal (1)
4. Choose **W**idth (4)
5. Type **.03** and press **Enter**
6. Choose **G**ray Shading (5)
7. Type **50** and press **Enter**
8. Press *Exit* (**F7**) to exit the Graphics:Horizontal Line menu
9. Press **Enter** to go to the next line

## Create the Rest of the Lines Using the Delete and Restore Keys

You could repeat this process nine more times, or you could copy the previous line and use **Ctrl-E** (if you are using the NEWSLETR keyboard) or **Alt-E** (if you are using the SHORTCUT keyboard) to make the adjustments. The following instructions show the keystrokes.

1. Position your cursor on the third line (on the [Hline:Full,Baseline,7.5",0.03",50%] code)

2. Press the **Delete** key twice (once to delete the [Hline:Full,Baseline,7.5",0.03",50%] code and once to delete the [HRt] code)

3. Press *Cancel* (**F1**), then **R**estore (1) (repeat both **C**ancel and **R**estore ten times—once to replace the line you deleted, the other nine times to make new lines)

   The following screen shows all the codes; your screen may only show the last few [HLine] codes.

```
Style: Press Exit when done                          Doc 1 Pg 1 Ln 2.43" Pos 0.5"
▓▓▓▓▓▓▓▓▓▓▓▓▓▓▓▓▓▓▓▓▓▓▓▓▓▓▓▓▓▓▓▓▓▓▓▓▓▓▓▓▓▓▓▓▓▓▓▓▓▓▓▓▓▓▓▓▓▓▓▓▓▓▓▓▓▓▓▓▓
[T/B Mar:0.5",.05"][L/R Mar:0.5",0.5"][Just:Left][Fig Opt][Fig: Box:1;DOLLAR.WPG;][HRt]
[Font:Univers Bold Italic (Scalable) 25pt][AdvToLn:0.705"][AdvToPos:2.87"] Deskto
p Publishing[HRt]
[Font:Univers Bold Italic (Scalable) 50pt][Color:Green][AdvToLn:1.1"][AdvToPos:2
.97"]News Review[HRt]
[Color:Black][AdvToLn:1.2"][AdvToPos:2.87"]News Review[Font:Univers (Scalable) 1
0pt][HRt]
[HRt]
[Hline:Full,Baseline,7.5",0.013",100%][HRt]
[Hline:Full,Baseline,7.5",0.03",70%][HRt]
[Hline:Full,Baseline,7.5",0.03",50%][HRt]
[Hline:Full,Baseline,7.5",0.03",50%][HRt]
[Hline:Full,Baseline,7.5",0.03",50%][HRt]
[Hline:Full,Baseline,7.5",0.03",50%][HRt]
[Hline:Full,Baseline,7.5",0.03",50%][HRt]
[Hline:Full,Baseline,7.5",0.03",50%][HRt]
[Hline:Full,Baseline,7.5",0.03",50%][HRt]
[Hline:Full,Baseline,7.5",0.03",50%][HRt]
[Hline:Full,Baseline,7.5",0.03",50%][HRt]
[Hline:Full,Baseline,7.5",0.03",50%][HRt]
▓
```

**NOTE:** When moving your cursor down (↓), up (↑), or right (→) on or between codes, WordPerfect sometimes jumps over codes and places your cursor on the text or a hard return. Moving your cursor to the left (←), however, will move one code at a time.

### Change the Attributes of the Fourth Line (Ln = 2.16")

1. Place your cursor on the [Hline] code to be changed; in this case, the fourth line

2. If you have the NEWSLETR keyboard, press **Ctrl-E**; otherwise press **Alt-E** (for Edit a code key)

3. Choose **G**ray Shading (5)

4. Type **30** and press **Enter**

5. Press *Exit* (**F7**) to exit the Graphics:Horizontal Line menu

### Change the Attributes of the Fifth Line (Ln = 2.19")

1. Place your cursor on the [Hline] code of the fifth line

2. If you have the NEWSLETR keyboard, press **Ctrl-E**; otherwise press **Alt-E**

3. Choose **G**ray Shading (5)

4. Type **20** and press **Enter**

5. Press *Exit* (**F7**) to exit the Graphics:Horizontal Line menu

### Change the Attributes of the Sixth Line (Ln = 2.22")

1. Place your cursor on the [Hline] code of the sixth line

2. If you have the NEWSLETR keyboard, press **Ctrl-E**; otherwise press **Alt-E**

3. Choose **G**ray Shading (5)

4. Type **10** and press **Enter**

5. Press *Exit* (**F7**) to exit the Graphics:Horizontal Line menu

## Change the Attributes of the Seventh Line
## (Ln = 2.25")

1.  Place your cursor on the [Hline] code of the seventh line

2.  If you have the NEWSLETR keyboard, press **Ctrl-E**; otherwise press **Alt-E**

3.  Choose <u>W</u>idth (4)

4.  Type **.1** and press **Enter**

    This line can be as wide (or tall) as you would like.

5.  Choose <u>G</u>ray Shading (5)

6.  Type **2** and press **Enter**

7.  Press *Exit* (**F7**) to exit the Graphics:Horizontal Line menu

## Lines 8 Through 12

Now reverse the process, making each succeeding line a little darker until the last thin black line by placing your cursor on the [Hline] code and proceeding as follows:

| | |
|---|---|
| Line 8<br>(Ln = 2.35") | Press **Ctrl-E** or **Alt-E** (depending on your soft keyboard), choose <u>G</u>ray Shading (5), type **10** and press **Enter**, press *Exit* (**F7**) |
| Line 9<br>(Ln = 2.38") | Press **Ctrl-E** or **Alt-E** (depending on your soft keyboard), choose <u>G</u>ray Shading (5), type **20** and press **Enter**, press *Exit* (**F7**) |
| Line 10<br>(Ln = 2.41") | Press **Ctrl-E** or **Alt-E** (depending on your soft keyboard), choose <u>G</u>ray Shading (5), type **30** and press **Enter**, press *Exit* (**F7**) |
| Line 11<br>(Ln = 2.44") | Press **Ctrl-E** or **Alt-E** (depending on your soft keyboard), choose <u>G</u>ray Shading (5), type **50** and press **Enter**, press *Exit* (**F7**) |
| Line 12<br>(Ln=2.47") | Press **Ctrl-E** or **Alt-E** (depending on your soft keyboard), choose <u>G</u>ray Shading (5), type **70** and press **Enter**, press *Exit* (**F7**) |

Press **Home**, **Home**, **Down Arrow** (↓) to place your cursor beyond the [HRt] code

```
Style: Press Exit when done                              Doc 1 Pg 1 Ln 2.5" Pos 0.5"

[T/B Mar:0.5",.05"][L/R Mar:0.5",0.5"][Just:Left][Fig Opt][Fig: Box:1;DOLLAR.WPG;][HRt]
[Font:Univers Bold Italic (Scalable) 25pt][AdvToLn:0.705"][AdvToPos:2.87"] Deskto
p Publishing[HRt]
[Font:Univers Bold Italic (Scalable) 50pt][Color:Green][AdvToLn:1.1"][AdvToPos:2
.97"]News Review[HRt]
[Color:Black][AdvToLn:1.2"][AdvToPos:2.87"]News Review[Font:Univers (Scalable) 1
0pt][HRt]
[HRt]
[Hline:Full,Baseline,7.5",0.013",100%][HRt]
[Hline:Full,Baseline,7.5",0.03",70%][HRt]
[Hline:Full,Baseline,7.5",0.03",50%][HRt]
[Hline:Full,Baseline,7.5",0.03",30%][HRt]
[Hline:Full,Baseline,7.5",0.03",20%][HRt]
[Hline:Full,Baseline,7.5",0.03",10%][HRt]
[Hline:Full,Baseline,7.5",0.1",2%][HRt]
[Hline:Full,Baseline,7.5",0.03",10%][HRt]
[Hline:Full,Baseline,7.5",0.03",20%][HRt]
[Hline:Full,Baseline,7.5",0.03",30%][HRt]
[Hline:Full,Baseline,7.5",0.03",50%][HRt]
[Hline:Full,Baseline,7.5",0.03",70%][HRt]
```

## The Last Thin Black Line (Ln = 2.5")

1. Press *Graphics* (**Alt-F9**)

2. Choose **L**ine (5)

3. Choose **H**orizontal (1)

4. Press *Exit* (**F7**) to exit the Graphics:Horizontal Line menu
   This will keep the standard black hairline defaults.

5. Press **Enter** to go to the next line

```
Style: Press Exit when done                              Doc 1 Pg 1 Ln 2.52" Pos 0.5"

[Hline:Full,Baseline,7.5",0.03",50%][HRt]
[Hline:Full,Baseline,7.5",0.03",70%][HRt]
[Hline:Full,Baseline,7.5",0.013",100%][HRt]
```

## Placement of the Dateline Text

Use your ruler to measure the space where you want your dateline text to appear.

1. Press *Format* (**Shift-F8**)

2. Choose **O**ther (4)

3. Choose **A**dvance (1)

4. Choose L**i**ne (3)

5. Type **2.26** and press **Enter**

   **NOTE:** I started with 2.25, then after viewing, pressed **Ctrl-E** (the edit code key) while my cursor was on the [AdvToLn] code, and adjusted the line down to 2.26.

6. At Selection: <u>0</u>, press *Exit* (**F7**) to exit the Format:Other menu

   **NOTE:** I preferred to have the text in four spaces, but you might like yours flush against the margin.

7. Type **January 1, 1993**

8. Press *Flush Right* (**Alt-F6**)

9. Type **Volume 1, Number 1** (spaces optional)

## Masthead Finale

1. Press **Enter** three times for blank lines

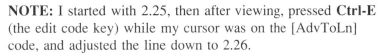

```
Style: Press Exit when done                          Doc 1 Pg 1 Ln 2.76" Pos 0.5"

[Hline:Full,Baseline,7.5",0.03",30%][HRt]
[Hline:Full,Baseline,7.5",0.03",50%][HRt]
[Hline:Full,Baseline,7.5",0.03",70%][HRt]
[Hline:Full,Baseline,7.5",0.03",100%][HRt]
[AdvToLn:2.26"] January 1, 1993[Flsh Rgt]Volume 1, Number 1 [HRt]
[HRt]
[HRt]
```

2. Press *Exit* (**F7**) to exit the Style (codes) screen

3. Press *Exit* (**F7**) to exit the Styles:Edit screen

4. Press *Exit* (**F7**) to exit the Styles screen

 **NOTE:** Do *not* turn the style on again or the masthead will appear more than once.

You are now at your editing screen (for the document), which appears blank except for a code in Reveal Codes. You might have to press **Home, Home, Up Arrow** (↑), or press **Home, Home, Down Arrow** (↓). Notice the status line (Ln = 2.76").

## Print View Your Accomplishments

1. If you have the NEWSLETR keyboard, press **Ctrl-P**; otherwise press *Print* (**Shift-F7**) and choose **V**iew (6)

2. Press *Exit* (**F7**) when finished

## Make Adjustments

Depending on your printer and font selections, you may have to make some position adjustments. If no adjustments are necessary, move to Headline.

1. Press *Style* (**Alt-F8**)

2. Move your cursor to Masthead

3. Choose **E**dit (4)

4. Choose **C**odes (4)

5. Place your cursor on the code to be changed

6. If you have the NEWSLETR keyboard, press **Ctrl-E**; otherwise press **Alt-E** (edit a code key)

# Headline

Press **Home**, **Home**, **Down Arrow** (↓) to position your cursor after all codes. Be sure your cursor is beyond the Masthead style. Using *Reveal Codes* (**F11**) or *Print:View* will sometimes cause your cursor to move.

You created an open style for the masthead, which means that any formatting code you entered will behave as if you had placed it in the document directly. In a paired style code, the codes surround the blocked text and are turned off again, leaving no effect on any text after the [Style Off] code. An example of a paired code is the [BOLD] [bold] code. An example of an open code is the *Format:Margin* code.

## Create a Paired Style for the Headline

1. Press *Style* (**Alt-F8**)

2. Choose **C**reate (3)

3. Choose **N**ame (1)

4. Type **Headline** and press **Enter**

5. Choose **T**ype (2)

6. Choose **P**aired (1)

7. Choose **D**escription (3)

8. Type **Universal, Bold, 24p, Center** and press **Enter**

9. Choose **C**odes (4)

   All codes should appear before the comment box.

### Select a Font, Center, and Turn on the Style

1. If you have the NEWSLETR keyboard, press **Ctrl-F**; otherwise press *Font* (**Ctrl-F8**) and choose **F**ont (4)

2. Move the cursor to Univers Bold (Scalable)

3. Choose **S**elect (1)

4. At Point size:, type **24** and press **Enter**

5. Choose *Center* (**Shift-F6**)

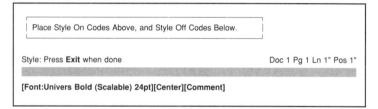

6. Press *Exit* (**F7**) to exit the Style (codes) screen

7. Press *Exit* (**F7**) to exit the Styles:Edit Menu

8. Choose **O**n (1)

   You should now be at the editing screen.

### Type the Headline

1. Type **Linking Your Spreadsheets and Graphs** and press **Enter**

2. Press *Center* (**Shift-F6**)

3. Type **What a Breeze !!** and press **Enter**

4. Press **Right Arrow** (→) to place the cursor on the outside of the [Style Off:Headline] code

5. Press **Enter** twice more to create extra white space

# The Graph

Create a spreadsheet and graph in your favorite spreadsheet program. Keep in mind the size of spreadsheet you want to link with WordPerfect. If the spreadsheet is too large, it won't be aesthetically appealing. Save the spreadsheet as usual.

Save the graph from your spreadsheet to a .PIC file in the WordPerfect Graphics directory, for example: C:\WP51\GRAPHICS\filename.PIC.

## Create a Border with the Shadow Effect

1. Press *Graphics* (**Alt-F9**)

2. Choose **F**igure (1)

3. Choose **O**ptions (4)

4. Choose **B**order Style (1)

5. Choose **S**ingle (2) for the left side

6. Choose **E**xtra Thick (7) for the right side

7. Choose **S**ingle (2) for the top

8. Choose **E**xtra Thick (7) for the bottom

9. Choose **O**utside Border Space (2)

10. Type **.167** and press **Enter** (repeat four times)

    **NOTE:** You could also type **12p** and press **Enter** (12p = .167").

11. Choose **I**nside Border Space (3)

12. Type **0** (zero) and press **Enter** (repeat four times)

13. At Selection: <u>0</u>, press *Exit* (**F7**) to exit the Options:Figure menu

## Link Your SpreadSheet Graph to WordPerfect

Place the graph from your spreadsheet before you turn your column mode on so the text will surround it. If you do not have a graph from your spreadsheet at the moment, use any graphic just so you can complete the exercise.

1. Press **Ctrl-G** for Graphics from either soft keyboard

 **NOTE:** This the same as pressing *Graphics* (**Alt-F9**), then choosing **F**igure (1), **C**reate (1).

2. Choose C**o**ntents (2)

3. Choose Graphic on **D**isk (2)

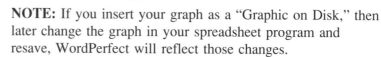 **NOTE:** If you insert your graph as a "Graphic on Disk," then later change the graph in your spreadsheet program and resave, WordPerfect will reflect those changes.

4. Choose **F**ilename (1)

5. Press *List* (**F5**)

6. Press **Enter**

7. Highlight your graph (.PIC) file
   In my case, BOOK.PIC

8. Choose **R**etrieve (1)

9. Choose Anchor **T**ype (4)

   Choose P**a**ge (2)

   Press **Enter** or 0 (do *not* skip pages)

10. Choose **V**ertical Position (5)

    Choose **S**et Position (5)

    Type **4.5** and press **Enter**

11. Choose **H**orizontal Position (6)

    Choose **S**et Position (3)

    Type **1.75** and press **Enter**

12. Choose **S**ize (7)

    Choose Set **H**eight/Auto Width (2)

    Type **1.5** and press **Enter**

13. Press *Exit* (**F7**) to exit the Definition:Figure menu

# Columns

## Define Your Column Widths and Turn on the Column Code

1. Press *Columns/Table* (**Alt-F7**)

2. Choose **C**olumns (1)

3. Choose **D**efine (3)

4. Choose **N**umber (2)

5. Type **3** and press **Enter**

   WordPerfect will create three identical width columns.

6. Press *Exit* (**F7**) to exit the Text Column Definition menu

7. At Columns: choose **O**n (1)

# The Table or Spreadsheet

You cannot retrieve a table in the column mode. You must put the table in a graphics box, then put the graphics box in or between the columns.

Even if you do not have a spreadsheet from another product, please continue. The instructions cover both linking your spreadsheet with another product and creating a table in WordPerfect.

## Options for Graphics Box That Holds the Table

1. Press *Graphics* (**Alt-F9**)

2. Choose **T**able Box (2)

3. Choose **O**ptions (4)

4. Choose **B**order Style (1)

   Choose **N**one (1) four times

5. Choose **O**utside Border Space (2)

   Type **0** (zero) and press **Enter** (repeat four times)

6. Choose **I**nside Border Space (3)

> Type **0** (zero) and press **Enter** (repeat four times)

7. At Selection: <u>0</u>, press *Exit* (**F7**) to exit the Options:Table Box menu

### Create the Table Box Graphic

1. Press *Graphics* (**Alt-F9**)

2. Choose **T**able Box (2)

3. Choose **C**reate (1)

4. Choose Anchor **T**ype (4)

> Choose P**a**ge (2)
>
> Press **Enter** or 0 for the number of pages to skip (do not skip pages)

5. Choose **V**ertical Position (5)

> Choose **B**ottom (4)

6. Choose **H**orizontal Position (6)

> Choose Columns (2)
>
> At Enter Column(s): type **2-3** and press **Enter**
>
> Choose **F**ull (4) to expand across both columns

WordPerfect should have adjusted the size for you; if not, the width is 4.83".

If you do not have a spreadsheet created from another product, move ahead to **\*Create Your Spreadsheet Within WordPerfect**

# Prepare to Link Your Spreadsheet

1. Choose **E**dit (9)

This is where you will create the link to your spreadsheet.

---

**Box:** press **Exit** when done. **Graphics** to rotate text.     Ln 0" Pos 0"

---

## Set Your Font Size

1. If you have the NEWSLETR keyboard, press **Ctrl-F**; otherwise press *Font* (**Ctrl-F8**) and choose F̲ont (4)

2. Move your cursor to Univers (Scalable)

   This is an easy font to read in small sizes.

3. Choose S̲elect (1)

4. At Point size:, type **10** and press **Enter**

## Set the Options for the Spreadsheet Link

1. Press *Text-In/Out* (**Ctrl-F5**)

2. Choose S̲preadsheet (5)

3. Choose L̲ink Options (4)

   **NOTE:** Update only when you are ready, not every time you retrieve the WordPerfect file; updating sometimes changes the format you had previously set up in WordPerfect.

4. Choose Update on R̲etrieve (1) = No

   This comment will not print out. The screen shows just the name of the file and that it is a linked file.

5. Choose S̲how Link Codes (2) = Yes

6. At Selection: 0̲, press **Enter** to leave the menu

## Retrieve the Spreadsheet and Create the Link

1. Press *Text-In/Out* (**Ctrl-F5**)

2. Choose S̲preadsheet (5)

3. Choose C̲reate Link (2)

4. Choose F̲ilename (1)

5. Type the name of the path and the filename of the spreadsheet, then press **Enter**

   For example: C:\DATA\QPRO\BOOK.WQ4

**NOTE:** If you don't want to use the whole spreadsheet, choose **R**ange (2) and then type the range of cells you do want, for example: E3..G14.

6. Choose **T**ype (3)

7. Choose **T**able (1)

8. Choose **P**erform Link (4)

## Change the Attributes of the Table

1. Move your cursor inside the table, to cell **A1**

2. Press *Columns/Table* (**Alt-F7**)

3. Choose **O**ptions (6)

4. Choose **P**osition (3)

5. Choose **F**ull (4)

6. Press *Exit* (**F7**) to exit the Options menu

   This will look cramped at first, but it will automatically spread out.

## Join the Top Row Cells to Make One Cell

1. Press *Block* (**F12**)

2. Press the **End** key to move the cursor to the last cell in the row to highlight the whole top row

3. Choose **J**oin (7)

4. Choose **Y**es

## Center the Title "Expenses"

1. Choose **F**ormat (2)

2. Choose **C**ell (1)

3. Choose **J**ustification (3)

4. Choose **C**enter (2)

5. Press *Exit* (**F7**) to exit the Table mode

### Exit back to Your Document

1. Press *Exit* (**F7**) to exit the Table Box Edit screen

2. Press *Exit* (**F7**) to exit the Definition:Table Box menu

If you have just linked your spreadsheet, move to **\*Create Three Vertical Lines**

# *Create Your Spreadsheet Within WordPerfect

1. Choose <u>E</u>dit (9)

   This is where you create your spreadsheet.

### Set Your Font Size

1. If you have the NEWSLETR keyboard, press **Ctrl-F**; otherwise press *Font* (**Ctrl-F8**) and choose <u>F</u>ont (4)

2. Move your cursor to Univers (Scalable)

   This is an easy font to read in small sizes.

3. Choose <u>S</u>elect (1)

4. Type **10** and press **Enter**

### Create the Table

1. Press *Columns/Table* (**Alt-F7**)

2. Choose <u>T</u>ables (2)

3. Choose <u>C</u>reate (1)

4. At Number of columns, type **5** and press **Enter**

5. At Number of rows, type **6** and press **Enter**

Each box is called a cell, and each cell has an address (A1, B4, E6). The columns are alphabetic (A, B, C, D, E) and the rows are numeric (1, 2, 3, 4).

## Expand and Contract Columns

1. Move your cursor to cell A2

   Press **Ctrl-Right Arrow** (→) to expand the column one character

2. Move your cursor to cell B2

   Press **Ctrl-Left Arrow** (←) three times to contract the column three characters

3. Move your cursor to cell C2

   Press **Ctrl-Left Arrow** (←) three times to contract the column three characters

4. Move your cursor to cell D2

   Press **Ctrl-Left Arrow** (←) three times to contract the column three characters

5. Move your cursor to cell E2

   Press **Ctrl-Right Arrow** (→) until the column has expanded to your specifications

## Change the Attributes of the Table

1. Move your cursor inside the table, cell **A1**
2. Press *Columns/Table* (**Alt-F7**)
3. Choose **O**ptions (6)
4. Choose **P**osition (3)
5. Choose **F**ull (4)
6. Press *Exit* (**F7**) to exit the Table Options menu

## Join the Top Row Cells to Make One Cell

Your cursor should be in cell A1.

1. Press *Block* (**F12**) or (**Alt-F4**)
2. Press the **End** key to move the cursor to the last cell in the row to highlight whole top row
3. Choose **J**oin (7)
4. Choose **Y**es

## Center the Top Two Rows

1. Press *Block* (**F12**) or (**Alt-F4**)
2. Press the **End** key, then **Down Arrow** (↓) to highlight the top two rows
3. Choose Format (2)
4. Choose Cell (1)
5. Choose Justify (3)
6. Choose Center (2)

## Center the Left Column

1. Move your cursor to cell A3
2. Press *Block* (**F12**) or (**Alt-F4**)
3. Press **Down Arrow** (↓) three times to highlight cells A3 through A6, the first column of cells
4. Choose Format (2)
5. Choose Cell (1)
6. Choose Justify (3)
7. Choose Center (2)

## Decimal Align the Cells That Will Contain Numbers or Formulas

1. Move your cursor to cell B3, the first cell you want decimal-aligned
2. Press *Block* (**F12**) or (**Alt+F4**)
3. Highlight all the cells to be aligned by moving to cell E6 (lower rightmost cell)
4. Choose Format (2)
5. Choose Cell (1)
6. Choose Justify (3)
7. Choose Decimal Align (5)

## Specify the Number of Decimals to Show

When calculating in WordPerfect, the result will show two decimal places unless you specify otherwise.

1. Move your cursor to cell B3, the first column where decimals will appear

2. Press *Block* (**F12**) or (**Alt-F4**)

3. Move your cursor to cell E3 to highlight all the columns to be formatted

4. Choose **F**ormat (2)

5. Choose Col**u**mn (2)

6. Choose # **D**igits (4)

7. At Number of decimal places, type **0** (zero) and press **Enter**

8. Press *Exit* (**F7**) to exit the Table Edit: mode

   You cannot enter data while in the Table Edit: mode because if you start typing letters or numbers, you will be selecting menu items instead of entering data.

## Type the Data in Each Cell

- To move to the left adjacent cell, press the **Tab** key
- To move to the right adjacent cell, press the **Shift-Tab** key
- To move to a lower cell, press the **Down Arrow** (↓) key

If you press **Enter**, the cell will become higher. If you pressed **Enter** by mistake, press the **Backspace** key now.

Because WordPerfect does calculations automatically, do not type any numbers in cells E3 through E6 nor in cells B6 through E6.

## Perform Calculations

1. Position your cursor in any cell in the table

    **NOTE:** If your cursor is outside the table, you will create another table instead of modifying the current one.

2. Press *Columns/Table* (**Alt-F7**) to return to the Table Edit: mode

## Add Columns

1. Move your cursor to cell B6, the cell where your column total will be calculated

2. Choose **M**ath (5)

3. Choose ± (4)

4. Move your cursor to cell C6

5. Choose **M**ath (5)

6. Choose ± (4)

7. Move your cursor to cell D6

8. Choose **M**ath (5)

9. Choose ± (4)

## Create a Formula

1. Move your cursor to cell E3, the cell where your row total will be calculated

2. Choose **M**ath (5)

3. Choose **F**ormula (2)

4. Type **B3+C3+D3** (no spaces allowed) and press **Enter**

## Copy the Formula Down

You could go to each subsequent cell and keep creating formulas, or you could copy the formula, which would then automatically adjust to the relative rows.

1. Keep your cursor in cell E3, the cell to be copied from
2. Choose **M**ath (5)
3. Choose Co**p**y (3)
4. Choose **D**own
5. Type **3** and press **Enter** to signify how many cells to copy down

## To Recalculate

Entries in the table can be changed at any time, but formula calculation is not automatic. You must *recalculate* the table, in some cases, more than once.

1. Make sure the cursor is in the Table Edit: mode
2. Choose **M**ath (5)
3. Choose **C**alculate (1)

## Make Table Adjustments

1. Use **Ctrl-Left Arrow** (←) or **Ctrl-Right Arrow** (→) to adjust the column width as necessary
2. Press *Exit* (**F7**) to exit the Table Edit: mode
3. Type a $ sign in any cell you want

## Exit back to Your Document

1. Press *Exit* (**F7**) to exit the Table Box: screen
2. Press *Exit* (**F7**) to exit the Definition:Table Box menu

# *Create Three Vertical Lines

## Print View

1. Press *Print* (**Shift-F7**)

2. Choose <u>V</u>iew (6)

3. Press *Exit* (**F7**) when you are done

---

Doc 1 Pg 1 Ln 3.82" Pos .05"

[Open Style:Masthead][Style On:Headline]Linking your Spreadsheet and Graphs[HRt]

[Center]What a Breeze !! [HRt]
[Style Off:Headline][HRt]
[HRt]
[Figure Opt][Fig Box:2;BOOK.PIC;][Col Def:Newspaper;3;0.5",2.67";3.17",5.33";5.83",
8"][Col On][Tbl Opt][Tbl Box:l;;]

---

## Create a Line Above the Graph Between Column 1 and Column 2

1. Press *Graphics* (**Alt-F9**)

2. Choose <u>L</u>ine (5)

3. Choose Create Line: <u>V</u>ertical (2)

4. Choose <u>H</u>orizontal Position (1)

   Choose <u>B</u>etween Columns (3)

   Type **1** and press **Enter** to place the line to the right of column 1

5. Choose <u>V</u>ertical Position (2)

   Choose <u>S</u>et Position (5)

   Press **Enter** to accept the default (3.82)

6. Choose <u>L</u>ength of Line (3)

   Type **.7** and press **Enter**

   Use your ruler; this may have to be adjusted.

7. Press *Exit* (**F7**) to exit the Graphics:Vertical Line menu

## Create a Line Below the Graph Between Column 1 and Column 2

1. Press *Graphics* (**Alt-F9**)

2. Choose **L**ine (5)

3. Choose Create: **V**ertical (2)

4. Choose **H**orizontal Position (1)

   Choose **B**etween Columns (3)

   Type **1** and press **Enter** to place the line to the right of column 1

5. Choose **V**ertical Position (2)

   Choose **S**et Position (5)

   Type **6.35** and press **Enter**

   Use your ruler; this may have to be adjusted.

6. Choose **L**ength of Line (3)

   Type **3.95** and press **Enter**

   Use your ruler; this may have to be adjusted.

7. At Selection: **0**, press *Exit* (**F7**) to exit the Graphics:Vertical Line menu

## Create a Line Between Column 2 and Column 3

1. Press *Graphics* (**Alt-F9**)

2. Choose **L**ine (5)

3. Choose Create: **V**ertical (2)

4. Choose **H**orizontal Position (1)

   Choose **B**etween Columns (3)

   Type **2** and press **Enter** to place the line to the right of column 2

5. Choose **V**ertical Position (2)

   Choose **S**et Position (5)

   Press **Enter** to accept the default of 3.82"

6. Choose <u>L</u>ength of Line (3)

   Type **4.26** and press **Enter**

   This may have to be adjusted.

7. At Selection:<u>0</u>, press *Exit* (**F7**) to exit the Graphics:Vertical Line menu

---

Doc 1 Pg 1 Ln 3.82" Pos 0.5"

[Open Style:Masthead][Style On:Headline]Linking your Spreadsheet and Graphs[HRt]

[Center]What a Breeze !! [HRt]
[Style Off:Headline][HRt]
[HRt]
[Figure Opt][Fig Box:2;BOOK.PIC;][Col Def:Newspaper;3;0.5",2.67";3.17",5.33";5.83",
8"][Col On][Tbl Opt][Tbl Box:I;;][VLine:Column 1,3.82",0.7",0.013",100%][VLine:C
olumn 1,6.35",3.95",0.013",100%][VLine:Column 2,3.82",4.65",0.013",100%]

---

# Create Styles for Shortcuts

## Create a Paired Style for the Subheadings

1. Press *Style* (**Alt-F8**)

2. Choose <u>C</u>reate (3)

3. Choose <u>N</u>ame (1)

4. Type **Sub-Head** and press **Enter**

5. Choose <u>D</u>escription (3)

6. Type **Universal, Bold, 14p, Centered** and press **Enter**

7. Choose <u>C</u>odes (4) to format the subhead

   You are now in the Style (codes) screen.

8. If you have the NEWSLETR keyboard, press **Ctrl-F**; otherwise press *Font* (**Ctrl-F8**) and choose <u>F</u>ont (4)

9. Move the cursor to Univers Bold (Scalable)

10. Choose <u>S</u>elect (1)

11. At Point size:, type **14** and press **Enter**

    You are now in the Style (codes) screen.

12. Press *Center* (**Shift-F6**)

103

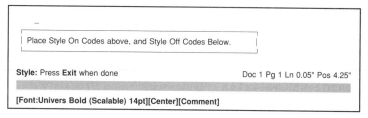

[Font:Univers Bold (Scalable) 14pt][Center][Comment]

13. Press *Exit* (**F7**) to exit the Style (codes) screen

14. Press *Exit* (**F7**) to exit the Styles:Edit menu

You will not use this style right now.

## Create an Open Style for the Regular Text

1. While still in the Styles menu, choose <u>C</u>reate (3)

2. Choose <u>N</u>ame (1)

3. Type **Regular Text** and press **Enter**

4. Choose <u>T</u>ype (2)

5. Choose <u>O</u>pen (2)

6. Choose <u>D</u>escription (3)

7. Type **CG Times, 12p** and press **Enter**

8. Choose <u>C</u>odes (4) to format the text

9. If you have the NEWSLETR keyboard, press **Ctrl-F**; otherwise press *Font* (**Ctrl-F8**) and choose <u>F</u>ont (4)

10. Move your cursor to CG Times (Scalable)

11. Choose <u>S</u>elect (1)

12. At Point size:, type **12** and press **Enter**

13. Press *Exit* (**F7**) to exit the Style (codes) screen

14. Press *Exit* (**F7**) to exit the Styles:Edit menu

## Use the Sub-Head Style for the First Subhead "Create Your Spreadsheet & Graph"

1. Move cursor to the Sub-Head style while still in the Style menu

2. Choose **On** (1)

3. Type **Create Your** and press **Enter**

4. Press *Center* (**Shift-F6**) to center

5. Type **Spreadsheet & Graph**

6. Press **Right Arrow** (→) to move out of the Sub-Head style code

   Your cursor was on [Style Off:Sub-Head]; now it should be beyond the [Style Off:Sub-Head] code.

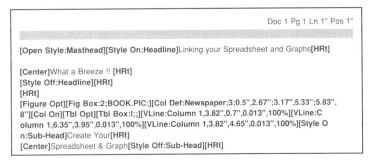

```
                                              Doc 1 Pg 1 Ln 1" Pos 1"

[Open Style:Masthead][Style On:Headline]Linking your Spreadsheet and Graphs[HRt]

[Center]What a Breeze !! [HRt]
[Style Off:Headline][HRt]
[HRt]
[Figure Opt][Fig Box:2;BOOK.PIC;][Col Def:Newspaper;3;0.5",2.67";3.17",5.33";5.83",
8"][Col On][Tbl Opt][Tbl Box:l;;][VLine:Column 1,3.82",0.7",0.013",100%][VLine:C
olumn 1,6.35",3.95",0.013",100%][VLine:Column 1,3.82",4.65",0.013",100%][Style O
n:Sub-Head]Create Your[HRt]
[Center]Spreadsheet & Graph[Style Off:Sub-Head][HRt]
```

7. After you are out of your Sub-Head style code, press **Enter**

   You press **Enter** after moving the cursor outside the Sub-Head style because the subhead has a larger font than the regular text. The white space between lines in a large font is larger than the white space between lines in a smaller font; therefore, move your cursor outside the style code to create a smaller white space.

## Use the Regular Text Style

1. Press *Style* (**Alt-F8**)
2. Move your cursor to Regular Text style
3. Choose **O**n (1)
4. Press **Enter** to create one blank line
5. Type the first text article for your newsletter column
6. Press **Enter** three times for two blank lines

## Use Your Sub-Head Style for the Next Subhead "Retrieve and Link"

1. Press *Style* (**Alt-F8**)
2. Move your cursor to Sub-Head
3. Choose **O**n (1)
4. Type **Retrieve and Link** and press **Enter**
5. Press *Center* (**Shift-F6**) to center
6. Type **in WordPerfect** then press the **Right Arrow** (→) to move out of the Sub-Head style
7. After you are out of the Sub-Head style, press **Enter** twice for one blank line

## Regular Text

WordPerfect treats each column as a separate page. When you want to end a regular page prematurely, press *Hard Page Code* (**Ctrl-Enter**). Do the same to end columns prematurely. To move from one column to the next, press the **Alt-Left Arrow** (←) or the **Alt-Right Arrow** (→).

**NOTE:** A paired style turns off the codes automatically, and an open style keeps the codes active.

1. Type the next text article for your newsletter column
2. When you are at the end of the text in the second column, press *Hard Page Code* (**Ctrl-Enter**) to force the cursor and text to the next column

### Use Your Sub-Head Style for the Next Subhead "Table Placement"

1.  Press *Style* (**Alt-F8**)
2.  Move your cursor to Sub-Head
3.  Choose **O**n (1)
4.  Type **Table Placement**
5.  Press the **Right Arrow** (→) to move outside the [Style Off] code
6.  Press **Enter** twice for one blank line
7.  Type the rest of the text for your newsletter

## Possible Problems

### If All the Text Does Not Fit or If You Have Too Much Space at the Bottom of the Page

1.  Calculate the distance to adjust
2.  Adjust the white space before or after your subheadings in styles
3.  Press *Style* (**Alt-F8**) to edit your Sub-Head style
4.  Move your cursor to Sub-Head style
5.  Choose **E**dit (4)
6.  Choose **C**odes (4)
7.  Press *Format* (**Shift-F8**)
8.  Choose **O**ther (4)
9.  Choose **A**dvance (1)
10.  Choose **D**own or **U**p to add or subtract white space where it will not be noticed
11.  Change the Regular Text style to a different-sized font
     For example: instead of using 11p, use 10.96, 11.02, or another appropriate size.
12.  Adjust the font size of your headline in styles

### If the Last Lines in Each Column Do Not Match

1. Calculate the difference

2. Adjust the leading after one of the subheadings using the Format:Other:Advance feature

3. If the columns are still not quite even, position your cursor on any of the [Advto__] codes, then

4. If you have the NEWSLETR keyboard, press **Ctrl-E**; otherwise press **Alt-E** to edit the code and type in a more appropriate number

## Make Adjustments to Even the Column Text

1. Move your cursor to the bottom line of the middle column

2. Notice the status line; in this case, Ln = 8.32"

3. Press **Alt-Right Arrow** ($\rightarrow$) to move the cursor to the third column

4. Place your cursor on the last line

5. Notice the status line again
   The example is 8.15"; the difference between 8.32 and 8.15 is .17

6. Press **Ctrl-Up Arrow** ($\uparrow$) to move your cursor one paragraph at a time to the first character of the first paragraph after the subhead Table Placement

7. For this paragraph only, advance down by pressing *Format* (**Shift-F8**); then choose **O**ther (4), **A**dvance (1), **D**own (2), type **.17** and press **Enter**

8. Press *Exit* (**F7**) to return to your document

## Make Adjustments to Lengthen the Vertical Line Between Column 2 and Column 3

The line started at 3.82 (base of first line) and should end at 8.32; the difference is 4.5 + .15 (the height of the text on the first line).

1. Place your cursor on the [VLine:Column 2,3] code

2. If you have the NEWSLETR keyboard, press **Ctrl-E**; otherwise press **Alt-E** (for edit a code key)

3. Choose <u>L</u>ength of Line (3)

4. Type **4.65** and press **Enter**

5. Press *Exit* (**F7**) to exit the Line menu

# Final Look

## A Final Look Before Printing

1. If you have the NEWSLETR keyboard, press **Ctrl-P**, otherwise press *Print* (**Shift-F7**) and choose <u>V</u>iew (6)

2. Choose <u>F</u>ull Page (3)

3. When you are ready to print, press *Cancel* (**F1**) to return to the Print: menu

4. Choose <u>F</u>ull Document (1)

## Save Your Newsletter Styles in a File

1. Press *Style* (**Alt-F8**)

2. Choose <u>S</u>ave (6)

3. Type **NEWSLINK.STY** and press **Enter**

4. Press *Exit* (**F7**) to exit the Styles menu

## Return to WordPerfect's Original Soft Keyboard

1. Press *Setup* (**Shift-F1**)

2. Choose <u>K</u>eyboard (5)

3. Choose <u>O</u>riginal (6)

## Save Your Document

# Notes

# Index

# About Crisp Publications

We hope that you enjoyed this book. If so, we have good news for you. This title is only one in the library of Crisp's best-selling books. Each of our books is easy to use and is obtainable at a very reasonable price.

Books are available from your distributor. A free catalog is available upon request from Crisp Publications, Inc., 1200 Hamilton Court, Menlo Park, California 94025. Phone: (800) 442-7477; Fax: (415) 323-5800.

Books are organized by general subject area.